From Conflict to Peace Building:

The Power of Early Childhood Initiatives

Lessons from Around the World

Paul Connolly and Jacqueline Hayden

with

Diane Levin

and the assistance of

Lisa Ruth Shulman, Contributing Reporter

Case studies were reported by:

Marta Arango

Duane Dennis

Eleanor Mearns

Siobhan Fitzpatrick

Ingrid Jones

Félicien Ntakiyimana

Ali Shaar

Kishor Shrestha

Radmila Rangelov-Jusović

Project management:

Pauline Walmsley

Healing Communities through Early Childhood Education
is a project of the World Forum Foundation
in partnership with NIPPA – The Early Years Organisation.

Masculine and feminine pronoun references in this book are used randomly for simplicity and in no way reflect stereotyped concepts of children or adults.

ISBN 978-0-942702-44-6
Exchange Press

ISBN 978-0-9542522-6-7
NIPPA – The Early Years Organisation

Printed in the United States of America
with gratitude for the support from the Bernard Van Leer Foundation.

The project was generously supported by:
The Social Justice and Social Change Research Centre, University of Western Sydney
and the School of Education at Queen's University Belfast.

Cover Photograph by Nancy Lessard
www.nancylessard.com

Table of Contents

Introduction

The effects of conflict on young children

Over the last century the nature of war and armed conflicts around the world has changed dramatically. While civilians used to represent the innocent casualties of war, they have increasingly become its target. During the First World War, for example, civilians accounted for just 14 percent of all deaths. By the Second World War this had risen to about 50 percent and in all subsequent wars civilians have accounted for at least 80 percent of all casualties (Cairns, 1996: 2). More recently it has been estimated that this figure has now reached over 90 percent (Machel, 2000; Save the Children, 2006; UNICEF, 2006).

Within this, children have paid a heavy price. During the last decade, best estimates suggest that around two million children were killed in wars and six million were mutilated (United Nations, 2006). A further one million were orphaned, 12 million were displaced and left homeless and 10 million permanently marked by "irreparable psychological and spiritual scars" (Fulci, 1998). At any one time, around 300,000 children are being used as child soldiers (Machel, 2000). It would seem, therefore, that rather than children just being caught in the crossfire, they are increasingly becoming the targets of war and armed conflict.

For some warring groups the murder, mutilation, and violation of children is justified in terms of children being seen as the "enemies of tomorrow" (Machel, 1996). "To kill big rats, you have to kill the little rats" was how one political commentator explained it during a radio broadcast shortly before ethnic violence erupted in Rwanda in 1994 (MacCormak, 1999). For others, this view of children as the "enemies of tomorrow" has led to strategies aimed explicitly at abducting and indoctrinating children. In relation to Uganda, for example, it has been reported that around 10,000 children were kidnapped from schools and villages and taken over to Sudan for indoctrination (Andvig, 2000). Similarly in Nepal, between the months of January and August 2005 some 11,800 children were abducted from rural schools by rebels "for political indoctrination or forced recruitment into the militia" (Save the Children, 2006: 6).

Unfortunately, and as worrying as all this is, it is actually only part of the picture. While children suffer acutely from the direct effects of war, they also tend to be disproportionately represented among the victims of its indirect effects. Armed conflicts decimate nations and ravage communities. They can often lead to the breakdown of the very fabric and infrastructure of societies and the interruption and sometimes complete loss of key services, such as the provision of education, housing and health, and the supply of food (Francis, 2006). In fact, these services are often among the first targets for those engaged in armed conflict. If children do not suffer directly at the hands of conflict, therefore, the likelihood is that they may well be affected indirectly to some degree by the breakdown of communities, the loss or impoverishment of public services and, in the most severe cases, through poor health, malnutrition and/or starvation (Machel, 1996; MacCormak, 1999). Moreover, even when armed conflicts have ended, children still have to deal with the legacy of the deep divisions that often remain, including the hatred, fear and mistrust that are often associated with these conflicts (Marshall, 2005a).

Purpose of this book

Just what is it like working as an early years professional within contexts such as these? What are some of the problems, issues, and challenges that one has to deal with when working with young children and their carers in societies affected by conflict? Most importantly, what can early years providers actually do in situations like these? How can they effectively meet the needs of children and their carers and what role can they play within their wider communities to help build peace? These are some of the key questions that will be addressed by this book when we hear first-hand from early years professionals around the world who are working in societies affected by conflict.

While some of the stories are shocking and upsetting, they are, above all, stories of hope and encouragement and of just what early childhood practitioners can do and achieve in the face of adversity. What each of the stories from around the world shows is that it is possible to make a real difference to the lives of children and families in societies affected by conflict. Moreover, the stories illustrate the power of the early years sector, not only as a foundation stone upon which to re-build communities, but also as a vehicle for peace building, because of its ability to reach across political divides and to encourage the differing sides in conflict to develop alternative visions of the future based around the needs of children.

This book has its origins in an event held in Belfast, Northern Ireland in 2004. The event, the Working

Forum Belfast, was organised jointly by NIPPA – The Early Years Organisation and the World Forum Foundation. It brought together early years professionals and researchers from 15 different countries around the world affected by conflict and provided the opportunity for them to share their stories, experiences, and perspectives. What soon became apparent to the participants was that while each of their situations was unique, the concerns they had regarding the effects of conflict on children and their families were remarkably similar.

Following the Working Forum Belfast conference "Building Bridges: Healing Communities through Early Childhood Education" held November 17-20, 2004 in Belfast, Northern Ireland, the participants have been able to continue sharing their experiences and working together and the result has been the creation of the International Working Group on Peace Building with Young Children (see: www.peacebuildingwithyoungchildren.org). This Working Group is a global initiative by early childhood practitioners, researchers, and civil society organisations to make visible the role of early childhood development as a force for reconciliation and peace building in regions experiencing or emerging out of armed conflict. This present book represents one of the first outcomes from the International Working Group.

Outline of the book

The book begins, in Chapter 1 with an outline of what existing research tells us about the impacts of armed conflict on young children and the key issues that this raises for early years educators working in such situations. This, in turn, provides the context for the next eight chapters that provide stories from early childhood practitioners working in regions affected by conflict. Each chapter begins by describing briefly the nature of the conflict in their region and the effects this is having on children and families. This is then followed by an outline of the work they are doing to begin addressing some of these effects, and each chapter concludes with reflections on the lessons learned from these initiatives to date. Chapter 10 draws together these chapters and highlights the key issues emerging from these differing contexts for early childhood practitioners working in conflict-affected regions. The final chapter, Chapter 11, describes the development of the International Working Group on Peace Building with Young Children, its current mission and goals, and how you can get involved.

How to contact us

Above all, this is a book of encouragement that we hope will provide practical support to those working in conflict-affected regions as well as inspiration to join and participate in the International Working Group. If you are moved by anything you read in this book, would like to know more about the Working Forum Belfast and/or would like to share your own experiences then we would love to hear from you. Please contact us via the International Working Group's web site at: www.peacebuildingwithyoungchildren.org.

Los efectos de los conflictos en niños pequeños

Durante el siglo pasado la naturaleza de la guerra y de los conflictos armados en el mundo cambio de manera dramática. La población civil que anteriormente era victima inocente ocasional, se ha convertido en su objetivo. Durante la primera guerra mundial, por ejemplo, la población civil representó solo del 14 porciento de todas las muertes. Durante la Segunda Guerra Mundial este porcentaje se elevo al 50 porciento, y en las guerras siguientes los civiles han sido al menos el 80 porciento de las victimas. (Cairns, 1996: 2). Mas recientemente se ha estimado que esta cifra ha alcanzado el 90 porciento (Machel, 2000; Save the Children, 2006; UNICEF, 2006).

Dentro de esta población, los niños y niñas han pagado un alto precio. Durante la última década, los estimativos sugieren que alrededor de dos millones de niños/as murieron en guerras y seis millones sufrieron mutilaciones. (United Nations, 2006). Un millón mas quedaron huérfanos, 12 millones sufrieron desplazamientos y quedaron sin hogar y 10 millones fueron marcados por "heridas psicológicas y espirituales irreparables" (Fulci, 1998). Alrededor de 300,000 niños están siendo usados como soldados (Machel, 2000).

Parecería que los niños y niñas se encuentran atrapados en el fuego cruzado, y que de manera creciente se están convirtiendo en objetivos de guerra y del conflicto armado. Para algunos grupos en guerra, el asesinato, mutilación y violación de niños esta justificado debido a que se ve a la niñez como "los enemigos del mañana" (Machel, 1996). "Para matar ratas grandes, tienes que matar ratas pequeñas" fue la explicación de un comentarista político en una emisión radial poco antes de que surgiera la violencia étnica en Ruanda en 1994 (MacCormak, 1999). Para otros, esta visión de la niñez como los "enemigos del mañana" ha llevado a estrategias con el propósito especifico de secuestrar o indoctrinar a los niños.

En relación con Uganda, por ejemplo, se ha reportado que alrededor de 10.000 niños han sido secuestrados de los colegios y las poblaciones y llevados al Sudan para endoctrinacion (Andvig, 2000). De manera similar en Nepal, entre enero y Agosto del 2005 alrededor de 11,800 niños fueron secuestrados de los colegios rurales por rebeldes para "endoctrinacion política o reclutamiento forzado a las milicias" (Save the Children, 2006: 6).

Desafortunadamente, con todo lo preocupante que es esto, solo es una parte de la situación. Aun cuando los niños sufren de manera aguda los efectos directos de la guerra también tienden a estar altamente representados entre las victimas de sus efectos indirectos.

Los conflictos armados diezman naciones y arrasan comunidades. Frecuentemente pueden llevar al rompimiento del tejido y la infraestructura de las sociedades, y a la interrupción o perdida total de servicios claves tales como la educación, la vivienda, la atención a la salud y la provisión de alimentos. (Francis, 2006).

De hecho estos servicios están entre los primeros blancos de aquellos que están involucrados en el conflicto armado. Si los niños y niñas no sufren directamente con el conflicto, es muy probable que se afecten indirectamente por el rompimiento de sus comunidades, de los servicios públicos, y en casos más severos a través de problemas de salud, desnutrición o hambruna. (Machel, 1996; MacCormak, 1999).

Más aun, después de que los conflictos armados han terminado, los niños aun enfrentaran el legado de hondas divisiones, el odio, el miedo y la desconfianza asociados con estos. (Marshall, 2005a).

¿Con estas consideraciones, como es, para un profesional que atiende a la niñez temprana trabajar en contextos como estos? ¿Cuales son algunos de los problemas, asuntos y retos que se tiene que enfrentar trabajando con niños y niñas pequeños y con sus cuidadores, en sociedades afectadas por el conflicto? Aun mas importante, ¿que pueden hacer realmente estos trabajadores en situaciones como estas? ¿Como pueden llenar de manera efectiva las necesidades de los niños y sus ciudadores y papel pueden desempeñar en las comunidades para ayudar a construir la paz? Estas son algunas de la preguntas claves a las que se referirá este libro, en la medida en que escucharemos de primera mano de los profesionales que trabajan con la niñez temprana afectada por el conflicto alrededor del mundo. Aun cuando algunas de las historias son chocantes y entristecedoras, son por encima de todo historias de esperanza y valentía sobre lo que los profesionales

que trabajan con la niñez pueden lograr enfrentando la adversidad. Lo que muestran cada una de las historias es que es posible hacer una diferencia real en las vidas de los niños y niñas y en sus familias dentro de sociedades afectadas por el conflicto. Mas aun, las historias ilustran el poder del sector que trabaja con la temprana infancia, no solo como cimiento sobre el cual se pueden reconstruir las comunidades, sino también como vehiculo para la reconstrucción de la paz, a través de su capacidad de cruzar las divisiones políticas y estimular a los sectores en conflicto para que desarrollen visiones alternativas del futuro, con base en las necesidades de los niños y niñas.

Este libro tiene su origen en un evento llevado a cabo en Belfast, Irlanda del Norte, durante el 2004. El evento, el Foro Mundial de Belfast, fue organizado de manera conjunta por NIPPA – La Organización para la Niñez Temprana, y la Fundación Foro Mundial. Participaron profesionales e investigadores que trabajan con la niñez temprana de 15 países diferentes afectados por el conflicto, y proporciono la oportunidad para que compartieran sus experiencias, sus historias y perspectivas. Muy pronto se hizo evidente para los participantes que aun cuando cada una de sus situaciones es única, las preocupaciones relativas a los efectos del conflicto en los niños y niñas y sus familias eran muy similares.

Como seguimiento al Foro Mundial Belfast en al 2004, los participantes han podido continuar el intercambio de experiencias y trabajar juntos, como resultado se ha creado el Grupo Internacional de Trabajo en Construcción de Paz y Niñez Temprana. Este grupo de trabajo es una iniciativa global de trabajadores con la temprana infancia, investigadores, y la sociedad civil para hacer visible el rol del trabajo en desarrollo infantil temprano como una fuerza para la reconciliación y la construcción de paz en regiones emergentes del conflicto armado.

(Más detalles sobre el grupo)

El libro inicia en el capitulo 1 con un esquema sobre lo que la investigación existente nos dice acerca del impacto del conflicto armado en la temprana infancia y las asuntos claves que emergen para los educadores que trabajan en tales situaciones.

Esto provee el contexto para los siguientes ocho capítulos que presentan las historias de los trabajadores por la temprana infancia en diferentes regiones afectadas por el conflicto.

Cada capitulo inicia describiendo brevemente la naturaleza del conflicto en su región y los efectos que esto tiene en los niños, niñas y sus familias. Continúa por una descripción esquemática de su trabajo para iniciar la referencia a algunos de los efectos, cada capitulo concluye con las reflexiones sobre las lecciones aprendidas a partir de estas iniciativas hasta la fecha. En el Capitulo 10, a partir de los capítulos anteriores, se relevan los aspectos claves que emergen para los trabajadores con la niñez temprana, a partir de las experiencias en estos diferentes contextos en áreas afectadas por el conflicto.

El Capitulo final, el Capitulo 11, describe el desarrollo del Grupo Internacional de Trabajo en Construcción de Paz y Niñez Temprana, su misión y objetivos, y como usted puede involucrarse. Ante todo este libro pretende ser un estimulo que esperamos pueda proporcionar apoyo practico a aquellos que trabajan en regiones afectados por el conflicto, así como inspiración para unirse y participar en el grupo de trabajo. Si usted queda motivado al leer este libro y/o quiere compartir sus experiencias nos encantara escuchar de usted y nos gustaría que conociera más acerca del grupo de trabajo: www.peacebuildingwithyoungchildren.org.

Chapter One

The Impact of Conflict on Young Children, Their Families, and Communities

The purpose of this first chapter is to provide the broader context for the stories that follow. It sets out what the research tells us about the impacts of armed conflict on young children and the key issues that this raises for early childhood practitioners working in areas affected by conflict. In the first part of the chapter we will briefly examine what some of the effects of armed conflict are on communities and families; then, in the second part of the chapter, examining how these impact directly on young children's health and well-being. The chapter concludes with a summary of the key issues raised by all of this for early years professionals that will, in turn, provide the core themes that run through the chapters to follow.

The impact of war and armed conflicts on communities and families

As already mentioned, the nature of wars and armed conflicts has changed. These days they are much less likely to be characterised by contests between countries and much more likely to involve armed conflicts between two or more warring factions within particular countries. In some places the army may be in conflict with civilians while in others there may be two or more groups of armed civilians fighting one another (UNICEF, 1996). These types of civil war are therefore often played out in communities, with villages, towns, and cities not only providing the backdrop to armed conflict but also often the actual focus of the conflict. As Harvey

El Impacto de los Conflictos en los Niños Pequeños y sus Familias y Comunidades

El propósito de este primer capitulo es proporcionar el contexto mas amplio para las historias que siguen a continuación. Presenta lo que los hallazgos de investigaciones nos dicen sobre el impacto del conflicto armado en los niños y niñas pequeños, y señalan asuntos claves que de allí surgen para los profesionales que trabajan con la temprana infancia en áreas afectadas por el conflicto. En la primera parte del capitulo examinaremos brevemente cuales son algunos de los efectos del conflicto armado en las comunidades y las familias, antes entrar en la segunda parte del capitulo donde examinemos como el conflicto afecta directamente la salud y bienestar de los pequeños. El capitulo concluye con un resumen de los asuntos claves para los profesionales que trabajan con la temprana infancia, los cuales también proporcionan el hilo conductor para los capítulos siguientes.

(2003: 5) has observed, for example: "violence against the civilian population by both government and non-state forces is now the rule rather than the exception, with civilians often being deliberately targeted in military campaigns."

The effects of all this varies dramatically from one conflict situation to the next, as the chapters to follow will demonstrate. At its most extreme form there is the brutal practice of "ethnic cleansing" whereby whole communities are wiped out either through mass slaughter or through being forced to leave their homes and land. It is estimated that at the end of 2003 armed conflicts had turned around 11.5 million people into refugees and asylum seekers worldwide with a further 25 million people having become "internally displaced" (Maxted, 2003). The plight for refugees can be severe — often having to walk for days without food or water and being vulnerable to further attack (Fulci, 1998). When they do arrive in a new and relatively safe place, they often face further suffering. In South Africa, for example, Thomson (2001) has reported how families who may have arrived together can then be separated because of the lack of suitable accommodation for those without work. In addition, they can also become "the objects of hatred and wrath" from the local population (Thomson, 2001: 183).

Those living in refugee camps remain at risk of harm and have few supports or safety nets in place to rely upon. Lack of access to basic amenities can lead to poor health and malnutrition and can feed crime and violence within and around camps. In fact, and as Stohl (2002) has reported, the camps themselves may become militarised, "exposing children to specific threats and intimidation, including rape, injury, forced prostitution, slavery, as well as forced recruitment into armed service."

For those communities not displaced, their plight can sometimes be little better. There can be the constant fear of attack and the anxiety and trauma that this can bring. In some cases combatants will attempt to undermine communities by purposely attacking and

damaging local hospitals, schools, sanitation systems, and food and water supplies (Miosso, 1996). In the Kongor area of Sudan, for example, it is reported that a massacre of people and cattle led to the reduction of livestock from an estimated 1.5 million to just 50,000 (Machel, 1996). Public health can therefore become one of the most deadly consequences of conflict, compounded often by the short supply of medicines, the lack of health professionals forced to flee the areas concerned for their own safety, and the difficulties faced by those attempting to monitor public health (Stohl, 2002). As Djeddah (1996) explains:

"The risk of communicable diseases . . . is greatly increased in wartime due to displacement, malnutrition, and the breakdown of safe water supplies and sanitation systems. Deaths proliferate from diarrhoea and dehydration as well as from lethal outbreaks of dysentery and cholera. Acute respiratory infections, measles, typhoid, and malaria also exact a very heavy toll."

Overall, and as Marshall (2005b: 45) has claimed in relation to wars in Africa: "far more people die as a result of disruptions in essential production, exchanges, and health services and at the hands of armed marauders than die 'honorably' on the battlefields. Small wars tend to create enormous humanitarian disasters."

More generally, the relationship between poverty and conflict is deeply interrelated (Cairns, 1996). As described above, armed conflict can uproot and decimate local communities and force people into conditions where they struggle simply to survive. However, poverty and the hopelessness and desperation that this brings can also be the impetus for conflict. Research evidence from Lebanon, for example, found that it was the poorest families who were most likely to experience violence and report its negative impact upon their lives (Armenian, 1989; Bryce, et al., 1989). A very similar picture was also found in Northern Ireland where a strong correlation existed between the level of socio-economic deprivation experienced by local communities and the number of sectarian murders committed in those communities (Connolly & Healy, 2004).

Overall this leads to what Marshall (2005b: 56) has termed the "conflict-poverty trap":

"Our evidence suggests that political instability in African countries is strongly, negatively correlated with general issues of human security; provision of education, health, and basic social services; investments in commercial infrastructure; and expansion of modern communications and information technologies. This is the essence of a conflict-poverty trap."

Of course, whatever the level and intensity of the actual violence that is experienced, one of the deep psychological scars that remains is the hatred and fear that is often passed on from one generation to the next. For those who have witnessed the killing of family or friends or who are, themselves, carrying the physical scars of conflict, it is extremely difficult to move on from this. Even in societies where armed conflict has largely come to an end, such as Bosnia and Herzegovina or Northern Ireland, some communities are still forced to live with a level of insecurity and fear and the continuing threat of indiscriminate attacks from members of the neighbouring community. Moreover, research has suggested that it is not always necessary to have directly experienced or witnessed violence to be affected by it. The media can be an important source of information locally (Cairns, 1996) and has the potential to fuel resentment and fear further.

There are many ways in which these effects of conflict on communities can then impact directly on families. Obviously the most brutal impact is through separation and loss. Family members may be killed as a direct result of the conflict. For some of these their deaths may have resulted from being actively involved as a combatant in the conflict, including those acting as "child soldiers" (UNICEF, 1996; Stohl, 2002; Maxted, 2003; Francis, 2006). It has been recently estimated, for example, that over half of all

conflicts around the world currently make use of child soldiers under the age of five (Save the Children, 2006: 5). However, for others they may simply have been targeted as a member of a particular community or literally just "caught in the crossfire." In addition, families can experience loss through particular family members having to leave their homes and flee for their own safety (Maxted, 2003). Families can also be dramatically separated as whole communities are forced into exile. There are, for example, harrowing stories of desperate parents feeling they have no option other than to abandon their children so that they can run faster to evade oncoming opposing armed combatants (Ntakiyimana, 2005).

Families who may have fled their homes out of fear but have stayed together, often face significant financial hardship. In Uganda for example, large sections of the rural population were forced to move to urban centers for their own safety. Many of these ended up in IDP (internally displaced people) camps. This, in turn, had a significant impact on their ability to make a living, as they could often be separated from their farms and/or have to walk long distances each day to get to them. Moreover, much of the land surrounding these camps soon became subjected to intensive use and degradation (World Vision, 2004).

For those families who remain together, either in their original homes or after displacement, there is evidence of the acute stress and anxiety that living in the shadow of conflict can cause. In some cases this can lead to parents exerting excessive concern and control over their children's every movements out of fear for their safety (Kenny, 2001); and in other cases it can lead to harsher and more authoritarian parenting styles more generally (Bryce, et al., 1989) as well as severe depression and domestic violence (Thomson, 2001; Maxted, 2003).

Moreover, for those parents who themselves may be deeply affected and possibly traumatised, it can be very difficult for them to offer any meaningful help and support to their children. In fact it is possible for them to exacerbate the problems faced by their children by passing on their own fears and anxieties through, for example, being over-protective or holding anxious discussions with others from which the children are excluded (Cairns, 1996).

Having said all of this, families and the wider community can also represent essential avenues of support at times of conflict. While conflict situations can undermine and put families under severe stress, there are also times when some families can grow stronger in the face of adversity (Cairns, 1996). Research has shown that strong families can act as a "buffer to the long-term effects of trauma" and thus encourage and facilitate recuperation (Cairns, 1996: 63). Interestingly, even in situations where an individual may have lost all immediate family through conflict, the fact that they had experienced close and supportive family relationships previously has been shown to help them deal psychologically with their loss over the longer term (Ressler, et al., 1988). Moreover, the wider community has also been found to provide an important source of support for those dealing with the trauma and aftermath of war and conflict. A number of research studies have, for example, reported lower levels of trauma and other adverse psychological effects among young people who have remained within their original culture as compared to those who have been forced to live in a new country where the culture is very different from their own (Sack, et al., 1986). The implications of all of this in terms of the need to work with and support families and local communities, as well as addressing the immediate needs of children, will be considered later and will provide a theme running throughout the chapters to follow.

The impact of war and armed conflicts on young children

So what are the effects of all of this on young children themselves? How does growing up in a society affected by war and armed conflict impact directly on the health and well-being of young children? To answer this question it is useful to look briefly at three differing types of effect: the impact on young children's physical safety; the effects of post-traumatic stress on young children; and the broader effects of conflict on children's social and cognitive development.

The impact on young children's physical safety

Some of the key figures relating to the number of children dying as a direct result of armed conflicts around the world have already been mentioned. During some of the most intense conflicts, the figures are truly shocking. During the five-year period between 1982-1986, for example, 333,000 child deaths were recorded in Angola and 490,000 in Mozambique (Bellamy, 1986). However, and as also stressed earlier, brutal as it is, this is only part of the picture. If such conflicts do not kill children directly, there is a likelihood that they will be killed by the indirect effects of conflict. Young children are especially vulnerable to malnutrition and the types of communicable diseases outlined earlier (Guha-Sapir & Gijsbert, 2004; Moss, et al., 2006; Zwi, et al., 2006). While malnutrition affects all children, it is those children under the age of three who face the greatest risk of mortality, particularly though "wasting" (i.e., gradual weight loss and general physical deterioration) (Machel, 1996). Also, and as MacCormack (1999) has pointed out, "in poor countries, where children are already vulnerable to malnutrition and disease, armed conflict can increase death rates by up to 24 times."

In addition, rape and the sexual assault of girls and women have become an insidious part of many armed conflicts (UNICEF, 1996; United Nations, 2002; World Vision, 2004). It can often be used as a deliberate policy and "tool of ethnic cleansing and terror" (Harvey, 2003: 46; see also Ayalon, 1998). It has been reported that in some raids in Rwanda, for example, nearly every adolescent girl who survived the initial attacks was then raped by the militia (UNICEF, 1996).

Young children are also affected by this in two ways. First, while adolescent girls are more likely to be the targets of such assaults, it is not unknown for younger girls to also be targeted. Moreover, young children who were conceived through rape can find themselves ostracised by their own community, as well as having a higher risk of having contracted sexually transmitted diseases, especially HIV/AIDS (Ayalon, 1998).

The effects of post-traumatic stress on young children

Beyond these direct forms of physical harm inflicted on young children through war and armed conflict, perhaps the next most significant impact is the psychological scars caused by post-traumatic stress (Pearn, 2003). A survey conducted by UNICEF in 1996 in Rwanda found that nearly 80 percent of children had lost an immediate family member and as many as a third of these had actually been witness to the killings (MacCormack, 1999). Similarly, it has been estimated that around 90 percent of children who were aged two when the war in Bosnia started "saw a family member or friend die during the siege of Sarajevo and in the surrounding villages" (Armstrong, 2002). The impact of witnessing such violent loss on young children's psychological well-being is simply unfathomable (Ayalon, 1998). However, even those children who are not direct witnesses to violent acts can still experience considerable trauma as a result of the sudden loss of and/or concerns for a close family member (Cairns, 1996). Such suffering is compounded for many older children, as the loss of a significant adult in the family can result in them becoming the main caregivers and/or main opportunity for the family to generate income (Stohl, 2002).

Children's responses to such traumatic events have been found to vary significantly. Some children have been found to be extremely resilient, while others have displayed a wide variety of symptoms including: changes in personality and temperament; nightmares and sleep disturbances; bedwetting; excessive attachment to significant others; fainting; aggressive behaviour; lack of concentration; withdrawal and depression; hyper-vigilance; loss of memory; speech loss and other psychosomatic disorders (Pynoos & Eth, 1985; Thomas, 1990; MacCormack, 1999). What seems to be important in many cases in relation to a child's responses to traumatic events is not so much the event itself but their interpretation of it (Cairns, 1996). One of the implications of this for providing even young children the space to explore and make sense of the events that surround them will be considered shortly.

The effects on young children's social and cognitive development

Finally, it is not surprising to find that the more general social and cognitive development of young children is also likely to be affected by living in war zones and areas affected by armed conflict. A child's emotional development, particularly their sense of identity and self-esteem can be affected profoundly by the loss of a parent or other close family member and thus the loss of attachment that results (Ayalon, 1998). Some children will develop a deep sense of anxiety and insecurity, while others will find it very difficult to trust those around them and may harbour deep feelings of vulnerability (Macksoud, 1994). In addition, some young children will develop low self-esteem and self-worth and other negative psychological traits. In some cases these may be associated with a child's loss of language, identity, or culture as a result of being displaced and/or separated from their immediate family (Pearn, 2003; Bargo, 2005; Moss, et al., 2006).

It is also possible that young children's social and moral development can be affected by growing up in a society affected by conflict (Shulman, 2006). As Macksoud (1994) suggests:

"During wartime, children [may] experience a sense of 'betrayal' when they watch such authority figures as parents, teachers, or local heroes — those role models they have learned to trust and respect — repeatedly breaching the expected moral standards of behaviour. This deep sense of betrayal may affect the moral development of these children. Basic assumptions about what is right and wrong are thoroughly shaken."

Moreover, these role models and the divided communities and societies that young children live in and experience may also impact upon their attitudes towards themselves and others. Research from Northern Ireland, for example, has shown that even children as young as three are beginning to develop preferences for the political symbols and events associated with their own community. Within just a few years, and by the age of six, the research estimated that a third of children in Northern Ireland were aware of the ethnic divide that exists and which "side" they belonged to, and around one in six were making overtly prejudiced statements about "the other side" (Connolly, et al., 2002).

Moreover, violence can easily become a routine and normalised part of children's lives (Shulman, 2006). This can be seen, for example, in relation to a number of studies that have reported how children tend to recreate the violence and conflict that surrounds them in their play. Observational studies conducted in South Africa have found that "police raid games" were prevalent in children's games (Liddell, et al., 1993) while in Northern Ireland it has been reported that children as young as four and five "were spending considerable time erecting barricades in their playgroups and pretending to throw petrol bombs" (Cairns, 1996: 84). However, rather than seeing such activities as important ways in which young children are attempting to explore and make sense of the conflict that surrounds them, anecdotal evidence suggests that a tendency exists for adults to stop such games for fear of how they may look or where they may lead. This, in turn, tends to be part of a general silence that children experience in relation to the events surrounding them whereby little opportunity is provided for them to explore what they have seen and to express their feelings about it (Smyth, 1998; Murray, 2001). As Murray (2001) has argued, not having the opportunity to make sense of

what is happening around them can simply increase children's sense of powerlessness and vulnerability.

Finally, the evidence would suggest that children's cognitive development can also be restricted as a result of living in societies affected by conflict. Delays in the development of numeracy and literacy skills as well as critical thinking have been reported (Nicolai & Triplehorn, 2003) as has the tendency for children living in such environments to place less value on education and schooling (McCauley, 2001). Part of the reason for this is likely to be the fact that schooling can be severely disrupted during periods of violence and conflict (Djeddah, 1996) and especially early childhood education programs (Women's Commission for Refugee Women and Children, 2005). It is reported, for example, that only 6 percent of child refugees are enrolled in secondary school (Blair, 2004: 11). Moreover, it has been recently estimated that around 43 million children worldwide are being kept out of school because of conflict (Save the Children, 2006: 1). Clearly, the insecurity created by living in a society affected by conflict is likely to undermine the ability of young children to play, learn, and explore as confidently and securely as they would in other environments.

Key challenges for early years providers working in conflict-affected societies

So what are the key challenges for early years providers in societies affected by war and armed conflict? It may seem from the above outline that the impact of conflict on communities and families is so great that there is little room or hope for early years services. However, the chapters to follow will show that not only is there significant potential to make a difference in the lives of children and families affected by conflict, but a great deal of exciting and innovative work is already taking place. As will be seen, the stories to be recounted are provided by members of the International Working Group on

Peace Building with Young Children working in very different contexts and situations around the world. Inevitably, therefore, the particular issues and challenges they face will vary enormously. However, from the discussion provided in this chapter, it is possible to identify a number of core issues that transcend specific situations and thus represent key challenges for early years professionals wherever they are working. There are six of these that were identified by the International Working Group at its first meeting in 2004 as a means of focusing their efforts. Each of these is posed as a question below. The purpose of the chapters to follow is to show, through the real and personal stories of early years educators, just how we can begin answering these:

■ What support can we give to caregivers in helping them deal with the effects of violence in their children's lives?

■ How can we best listen to the voices of young children and help them to explore, in a safe environment, their experiences of conflict and the beliefs, fears, and anxieties that arise from these?

■ In situations where there are high and intense levels of violence, how do we go about meeting the needs of children when their families and communities are literally disintegrating?

■ How can we begin to work effectively with families and communities in the many different contexts created by political violence and armed conflict?

■ How can we be effective advocates for children living in conflict-affected societies?

■ What role can we, as early years professionals, play in terms of helping to build the peace?

Chapter Two

Albania:
Ingrid Jones' Story

Albania is a small, predominantly rural country in southeastern Europe that has been struggling since 1991 to overcome its historical isolation and under-development caused by over 40 years of living under Communist rule. It is one of the poorest countries in Europe and suffers from high levels of unemployment and poverty and a poor social and economic infrastructure. Albania also remains a very traditional country; reflected partly by the continuing adherence of some local people in the north of the country to the Kanun — a system of common law dating back 500 years. One element of the Kanun that has had a particularly damaging effect on families and communities are the "blood feuds" that allows for families to exact revenge when one of their own members is killed. This, in turn, has sometimes led to a spiral of killings as families fall into deadly feuds.

Since 2003, the Christian Children's Fund (CCF) in Albania has been involved in an ambitious project to develop early child care centers — known as the Garden of Mothers and Children Centers — in the north and northeast of Albania. These Centers have played a vital role in providing much needed education and support to young mothers, who often live in isolation due to the combined effects of poverty and fear associated with the blood feuds. Moreover, the Centers have also begun working with fathers and local communities more generally in terms of conflict mediation; providing an encouraging example of the power of the early years in addressing conflict and promoting reconciliation and peace.

In this chapter, Ingrid Jones tells the story of the CCF's work in Albania and the problems, challenges, and lessons learned in setting up the Garden of Mothers and Children Centers. Ingrid is the Country Director for CCF Albania and oversees the work of its 23 staff. She originally trained and

Albania:
La historia de Ingrid Jones

Albania es un país pequeño y predominantemente rural, situado en Europa Sur — oriental, que desde 1991 ha estado luchando por sobreponerse a su aislamiento y subdesarrollo histórico, con más de 40 años bajo un régimen comunista. Es uno de los países más pobres de Europa y sufre de altos niveles de desempleo y pobreza, y una infraestructura social y económica muy precaria. Albania continúa siendo un país muy tradicional, esto se refleja parcialmente por la adherencia continuada de alguna de la gente del norte del país al Kanun — un sistema de leyes que data de más de quinientos años. Uno de los elementos del Kanun, que tiene un efecto particularmente dañino para las familias y las comunidades son los "enemistades de sangre," que le permiten a las familias cobrar venganza si uno de sus miembros es asesinado. Esto ha conllevado a que algunas familias se involucren en una espiral de asesinatos.

Desde 2003, Christian Children Fund (CCF), en Albania se ha involucrado en un ambicioso proyecto para desarrollar centros de cuidado diario — conocidos como los "Jardines de las Madres y los Niños" — en el norte y el noreste de Albania. Estos centros han jugado un rol vital en proporcionar educación necesaria para apoyar a las madres jóvenes, quienes con frecuencia viven aisladas debido a los efectos combinados de la pobreza y el miedo asociado con las venganzas sangrientas. Aun mas, estos centros han comenzada a trabajar con los padres y con las comunidades locales en mediación del conflicto; proporcionado y estimulantes ejemplos sobre el poder que los primeros años de vida pueden tener sobre el manejo del conflicto, y la promoción de la reconciliación y la paz.

En este capitulo Ingrid Jones narra la historia del trabajo de CCF en Alabanza así como sus retos, problemas y las lecciones aprendidas con la experiencia de los "Jardines de las Madres y los Niños." Ingrid es la Directora de País para CCF en Albania y supervisa el trabajo de un equipo de 23 personas. Originalmente se entreno y se desempeño como trabajadora social por más de 10 años en Inglaterra, antes de iniciar su trabajo en el exterior en Rumania, Bulgaria y el lejano oriente de Rusia. Antes de llegar a Albania Ingrid también paso algún tiempo en Kosovo adquiriendo experiencia de campo trabajando con familias y comunidades que había sido separada por los conflictos y tensiones de tipo étnico.

worked as a social worker in England for over 10 years before working on a range of projects overseas in Romania, Bulgaria, and the far east of Russia. Prior to Albania, Ingrid also spent time in Kosovo gaining first-hand experience of working with families and communities torn apart by ethnic tensions and conflict.

Setting the scene: Albanian society

Albania is a very small country located in the western Balkans with a population of approximately 3.3 million people. There are the Adriatic and Ionian Seas on its west coast; and it is bordered by Montenegro, Kosovo, Macedonia, and Greece. It is a mountainous country, particularly so in the north and northeast where there is very little agricultural land able to grow things. The south used to be very productive for agriculture, fruits, and vegetables; but with the disappearance of state subsidized farms Albania now mainly imports its goods from other countries, particularly Macedonia, Greece, and Turkey.

There are three key factors that set the scene for our work in Albania. The first is poverty. Albania spent

over four decades under strict Communist rule that resulted in the country being relatively isolated from the rest of the world and as a result under-developed. While Communist rule ended in 1991 there is still the legacy of that under-development to be seen across the country. Medical care remains scarce, particularly in rural areas, and basic infrastructure such as road and rail networks are poorly developed. Around a third of Albanians currently live below the poverty line with half of these living in extreme poverty, subsisting on less than $1 per day (Barjaba, 2004).

While the capital of Albania, Tirana, might look like any other affluent European city at first sight, you only have to travel out to the suburbs of Tirana to find signs of poverty. These suburbs are where the majority of people have migrated over the last 15 years from the north in search of work. Here you will find many houses that look nice from the outside and yet they are built illegally and are very basic with relatively nothing inside them. It is a similar picture in the north as well with apartment buildings or people living in rural villages. The conditions are very poor. Most families will have a cow, maybe a sheep, some hens, and often a small piece of land where they grow vegetables and fruit, but very little else.

The second factor that is partly a consequence of the poverty is the high level of emigration from Albania. Just over a third of the entire workforce, about 35 percent, have left Albania in search of work elsewhere. Many of these are young men, and the majority have gone to Greece and Italy (Barjaba, 2004). Moreover, there is also trafficking of human beings, especially children, which has been a real concern. According to various reports the number of children being returned to Albania has decreased; however, it still remains a problem. People were going to Italy and Greece, particularly by boat, so now we have a ban on people using small vessels at sea. The situation in the north is different as the country is landlocked and there are few border crossing points. People can just cross the mountains, and so illegal migration, or unaccompanied migration of children as it is termed, is on a much bigger scale.

The third factor relates to what can best be described as the patriarchal nature of the society here. Men are definitely in control when it comes to politics, work, and the home. Albanian women, particularly in the north, manage the care of the children and the household chores, but are limited in their socializing and activities outside of their homes. Young children have limited opportunities to socialize with age related peers as provisions for leisure activities are missing. The only opportunity many children have to mix with others their own age is within the school environment. Adolescent males will gather on streets and hang around in groups, whereas teenage girls will remain in their homes.

The "blood feuds"

All of these factors described above tend to lead to the isolation of young mothers, particularly those living in rural areas. Unfortunately, this is compounded by what has commonly become known as the "blood feuds," which create high levels of anxiety and fear among those families affected by them and further exacerbate the isolation that some experience, as they either confine themselves and their children to the home for fear of attack or flee their home and village altogether.

Box 2.1   Fact file: Albania

- A relatively homogenous society with approximately 98 percent of the population being ethnic Albanians. Of the remaining 2 percent, the majority are Greeks with smaller numbers of Macedonians and Serbian-Montenegrins (Barjaba, 2004).
- One of the poorest countries in Europe. About a third of its income (34 percent) comes from agriculture and another third (32 percent) from the service sector. Only 13 percent comes from industry. A significant proportion of its national income (21 percent) comes from remittances from Albanians working abroad (U.S. Department of State, 2005).
- 35 percent of the labour force in Albania has emigrated in search of work, representing a quarter of the entire population (25 percent) (Barjaba, 2004).
- For those remaining, there has been a dramatic shift from rural to urban areas with the population in regions such as Kukes, Shkoder, and Diber falling dramatically. Many of those left are without or with very poor access to basic health and social services (UNDP, 2004).
- It is estimated that about a third of the children (35 percent) have abandoned school due to economic reasons. Non-attendance is a particular problem in rural areas (UNDP & SEDA, 2005).
- Because of its geographic location, Albania has been a country of origin, transit, and destination for people trafficking. It is estimated that more than 5,000 Albanian women and girls were trafficked into prostitution in the last decade (Ministry of Public Order, Albania, 2002).

The "blood feuds" represent one aspect of the common law called the Kanun of Lek Dukagjini that dates back approximately 500 years to a time before Albania had written laws and jurisdictions. The Kanun is still widely observed and gives guidance and rules governing marriage, birth, death, hospitality, and inheritance. The blood feuds are one element of this and involve the taking of blood to avenge the killing of a member of one's family. The cause of the killing can be a minor issue or a fight that got out of hand. The Kanun gives guidance on how the two families involved in the feud should behave towards each other and when it is permissible, according to the Kanun, that revenge may be sought. The first attempt may be made within 24 hours of the first killing or otherwise a period of up to 30 days truce may be agreed by both families. If an agreement is not made within the 30-day period, then the killing may recommence. Part of the code related to the blood feuds has encouraged the use of mediators — well respected men in the communities — to mediate between the two families in order to prevent further killings and to maintain the respect and honor of both families.

Aspects of the Kanun are based on honor and are linked to the role of men. Once a man has been killed, it follows that the perpetrator or another member of his family must be killed by the first family's members. Under the Kanun, you are not supposed to kill women or children, but sometimes these laws are not followed so strictly now. It is because of this that

Box 2.2   The effects of blood fueds on families

Hasan, aged 30, was known in his village for being quarrelsome and had made a number of enemies. One day he was involved in a fight with a driver named Demir. Demir was 35 and a father of four children. During the fight, Hasan took a screwdriver from under the seat of his tractor and stabbed Demir in the heart. Demir died.

Demir's two brothers immediately sought revenge and took their guns to kill Hasan. By the time they reached Hasan's house, he had fled. However, they found Hasan's 70-year-old father, Xhelal, and one of Hasan's nieces, Aishe, age nine. Under the Kanun, a person is permitted to kill anyone of the killer's family within the first 24 hours. For this reason when they realized that Hasan had fled, they killed his father in front of Aishe.

While the brothers were arrested, sentenced, and are now in prison, the families remain caught up in a blood feud. Demir's family does not consider the death of Hasan's father sufficient revenge for their own loss. They still believe they should kill a younger man. Reconciliation and mediation has been tried, but so far the families have not signed an agreement to bring an end to this feud.

Hasan's mother, his wife, and five children remain isolated in the home. Initially, they neither attended school nor the Garden of Mothers and Children Center out of fear. The Administrative Mother, the elders of the village, and members of the Fathers' Board of the Center visited the family and explained to them that according to the Kanun the children who attend school are not at risk of being killed. Following these discussions the children returned to school and to the Center.

Hasan's two sons attend the Garden of Mothers and Children Center and his wife is one of the women who assists in the daily activities of the Center. All five children are accompanied by relatives when they go to school or the Garden of Mothers and Children Center. They are fearful despite the assurances that they will be safe. Both sons ask frequently when their father will return and if he is dead or alive.

children, particularly male children, become isolated in their family homes for fear that they may be attacked. If the males of the immediate family are unobtainable or there are no males, then the avenging family may seek out the next male in the extended family. This could be an uncle or a cousin, anyone whose killing it is felt will cause the most effect and harm to the other family.

During the communist era the blood feuds were not prominent, as there was obviously a very strong state that ruled everything, literally down to what type of haircut you had. However, since the fall of communism and the lack of an effective law and order, people have resorted, particularly in the northern districts of Albania, to the practice of avenging the killing of their family members through the blood feuds.

Although blood feuds are unacceptable and against the current laws and legislation of Albania, very little appears to be done to actually arrest, charge, and punish the perpetrator(s) of the death(s). One of the reasons for this is that local police officers are likely to be connected to the families in some way or another. Therefore, if they were to take action, then that could also turn the killing onto their own family; so while they may well know it is going on and who is involved, there is a reluctance to act.

The impact on families and children

One of the results of these blood feuds is that they increase further the number of Albanians, particularly the men, who leave the country. As already mentioned, there is a large number who leave because of unemployment and poverty in order to find work elsewhere. However, there are others who have chosen to leave Albania for their own safety. Some of these still find it hard to escape danger and often have to keep moving to avoid being found. We know of families, for example, who have moved down from the north to the suburbs of Tirana to

escape the blood feuds, but who have still been followed and killed.

For those who remain, the effect of these blood feuds creates a sense of fear and anxiety and forces families into isolation in an attempt to protect themselves. We know in one locality, for example, there are 257 children who do not go to school, have limited socialization or contact with friends or peers, and are unable to take part in leisure activities. This also has knock-off effects on children's education, self-confidence, well-being, and health. For many families, the inability to work affects the family's income level adversely. Also, they cannot access any of the available health care systems because they are totally isolated. It is because of fear that most adult male family members do not leave their homes. Mothers and other female relatives often accompany the children to and from school; and if the children happen to be out unaccompanied, the family members worry about them until they are safely back. Moreover, the family that needs to avenge the death of their dead male relative may issue threats, which increases the anxiety level within the family.

These levels of isolation and confinement in the home, together with the general levels of poverty that exist, have two main effects on young children. First, it has a significant effect on their health. A good portion of the homes do not have sanitation and plumbed-in systems, so there are a lot of problems with both the lack of water and also water that is not safe to drink. This in turn leads to problems with diarrhea and respiratory infections. Nutrition is another problem in that many of the children in the north are malnourished, and that is obviously due to poverty and lack of certain foods. For example, many families only have the opportunity to eat meat on rare occasions.

Second, it has an adverse effect on the young children's education and general development. There is little opportunity for stimulation for the children at home, with many homes having no toys or books. While they will usually have a television, it is not really child-orientated. The main consequence of this

Box 2.3   The effects of blood feuds on children

Kalosh, a father of three children living in a small village, was shot in the street by a gang when visiting a nearby city. The police investigated the killing but were unable to find the perpetrators. Kalosh's widow and her three children went to live with Kalosh's parents. Eventually she left the home to marry another man and her children — Sanije, Sami, and Tefta — remained with their grandparents.

However, the killing of Kalosh had a deep psychological effect on their grandfather. He continuously searched for his son's killer and sought revenge for his death. Due to his grief, he was unable to appreciate the effect his threats for revenge and shouting had on his three small grandchildren. Sanije also suffered from the shock of the death of her father. Her grandfather's temper and repeated threats to kill her father's killers also made her speechless; and she began to show other symptoms of trauma, hiding behind walls and under tables and eating soil.

Tefta began to attend the Garden of Mothers and Children Center. Tefta came for the first time to the Center with her aunt. When her aunt began to explain the children's situation to the woman running the Center (known as the Administrative Mother), Tefta began to cry. It took some time to calm her down. The Administrative Mother began to appreciate the loss and the need for additional attention that Tefta required. Tefta presented as disoriented, speechless, and withdrawn wanted to keep in close contact with the Administrative Mother or hide behind her back. The Administrative Mother gave her individual time, care, and attention. But this was not enough; she also advised Tefta's aunt how to

behave and care for Tefta and her siblings. After several months, Tefta began to change and was less withdrawn and began to play and integrate more with the other children. Tefta's brother and sister attended the Garden of Mothers and Children Center in the holidays, and the Administrative Mother encouraged them to join in different games, so that they could socialize with other children. These activities helped the children to deal with the trauma of their father's death and also helped them to make friends and to know that there was a place where they could feel safe and warm.

A friend of Tefta's grandfather arranged for a pension for Tefta from a Kuwaiti NGO for orphans. Tefta and her grandfather traveled to Tirana, the capital of Albania, to make their request to the organization. At one of the busy crossroads in Tirana, Tefta's grandfather thought he saw one of the alleged killers of his son. Always confused and overwrought with the idea of revenge, he released Tefta's hand and ran towards the man. Tefta, scared by her grandfather's actions, ran after him. She was hit by a car and killed.

Now the family has two deaths to avenge. Sanije and Sami attend the local school. Sometimes, so that they can feel close to Tefta, they go to the Garden of Mothers and Children Center where she spent many happy times. They are frightened and worried about what the future holds for them. Their grandfather still wants only revenge and does not understand the needs of his grandchildren. In the evenings the children remain inside their home and do not play outside or with friends. Sadness has been such a large part of their lives.

is that you find very quiet, passive children, very often with what we would term delayed speech. They have never had pens, paper, or any instruments for anything creative, and they are very used to just doing exactly what they are told. Moreover, the isolation that many young mothers experience means that there is such a lack of information, lack of knowledge, and lack of awareness. They have not had the experience themselves of a stimulating and child-centered home environment and so inevitably this is now being passed on to their own children.

The situation is worsened by the lack of access to other mothers and to reliable information and health care services. Young mothers have little opportunity to improve their skills and learn about early child care and development, nutrition, common childhood illnesses and how to treat them. They are also denied the opportunities to learn how to provide a stimulating and positive home environment that encourages and supports the child's all-round development. Moreover, children whose families are caught up in a blood feud have the additional stress and trauma to deal with. Some children have directly witnessed their relatives being killed, while many more live in an atmosphere of tension, fear, and uncertainty.

The development of the Garden of Mothers and Children Centers

It was these combined effects of poverty, the isolation of young mothers in a patriarchal society, and the impact of the blood feuds on families that provided the context for CCF and its work in Albania. The idea of establishing the Garden of Mothers and Children Centers in the rural areas of north and northeastern Albania was to improve the accessibility of young children and their mothers to information, preschool education, and health services.

The project began in 2003 and was funded by the World Bank, UNICEF, and Christian Children's Fund

Inc. This project followed the successful introduction of 17 Centers in the suburban areas of Tirana in 2001. The suburbs are inhabited by migrants from the northern areas of Albania who began to migrate to the capital in the early 1990s seeking to improve their economic and family life. The settlements have little infrastructure and suffer from a lack of water, electricity, education, and health services. Low levels of education make it difficult for the adults to find employment, so the families are very poor.

The staff of CCF Albania began to assess which areas of the north and northeast districts of Albania would benefit most from preschool education. They did this by visiting the regional and district education and health directorates and local government authorities. What the assessment showed was that there had been a dramatic decline in the level of state crèches, kindergarten, and school provision for the rural areas. This demise had come about through the migration of families from the districts with a corresponding decline in the numbers of children and the depletion in the numbers of trained teachers and health professionals. Under the communist regime, teachers and professionals were placed by the state into schools, hospitals, and kindergartens. This was one method of guaranteeing full employment and also ensuring a high quality of services to the population.

Once it had been confirmed that there was a need for preschool education and that communities were willing to participate and contribute to the operation of social centers, a more in-depth assessment was undertaken in order to choose the locations. Community meetings were held to assess the response of the communities and to explain what was needed and what would be provided under the two-year project. Because of the patriarchal nature of Albanian society, these meetings tended to be dominated by men who represented the local government, commune heads, village elders, or the mayors of the municipalities. While we would have liked to approach women directly, it was important at this early stage to work with the men and show respect for their decision-making roles; otherwise our work would have been very difficult.

To facilitate men's participation in the development and management of the Centers we encouraged the formation of Fathers' Boards. These Boards were not just made up of fathers, but of men from a range of backgrounds and positions within the local community. Initially, we planned for three Fathers' Boards, one for each of the three districts of Kukes, Diber, and Tropoje. These Boards that were made up of representatives from all the communities with a Garden of Mothers and Children Center, soon decided that each Center should have its own Fathers' Board as well. As we started out with 30 Centers this led to us establishing 33 Fathers' Boards in total. Their understanding and concept of early childhood care and development was limited, but they did want their children to attend a kindergarten.

The locations to open the Garden of Mothers and Children Centers were chosen in relation to a combination of factors: the level of need; whether the community was able to support it by voluntary work, maybe decorating a building or flattening the land outside the Centers; and the availability of an appropriate space and a woman to manage the Center. Most of the Centers were set up in private homes where there was a spare room that would accommodate 25 to 30 children.

Each Center was managed by an Administrative Mother (usually the owner of the house), and five mothers to support her in the everyday activities of the Center. The Administrative Mother received a small fee from the project, but the other mothers volunteered. The Administrative Mothers and the volunteers were all trained by CCF staff to provide child-centered activities to develop the children's physical, emotional, intellectual, and social skills. Later, additional training was provided by the senior specialists from NIPPA – The Early Years Organisation based in Northern Ireland who further promoted the emphasis of learning through play. This emphasis was important, as the majority of the

mothers and women who took part in the child development training had very little appreciation that children could learn through play and expected their children to be taught reading, writing, and mathematics using rote and paper and pencils.

It was through these initial steps that we managed to encourage women and children to come to the Centers. To begin with, some fathers were hesitant and reluctant to participate, as they had not been exposed before this point to the work of NGOs or to the concepts of early childhood education and development. However, possibly because of the lack of trust, we saw a lot of men coming to the Centers at the beginning; but gradually their numbers have decreased as they saw what was actually going on in the Centers and thus they learned to trust CCF.

Since the end of 2005 the Garden of Mothers and Children Centers have been self-funding, which has been a big problem because of the lack of finance available to regional and district education directorates, municipalities, or communes. We would have liked and hoped that the Centers would be financed by the local communes or municipalities or the directorates of education. That has not happened because up to now Albania has not made preschool education the priority but is concentrating instead on mandatory education. Most of the Centers therefore run on very limited funding made up of: some contributions from parents, although this is very limited; some contributions through the directorate of education; and some through the local communes through a system of social assistance, where they are paying the Administrative Mother to run the Center. However, the long-term sustainability of these Centers is still questionable and their situation remains very precarious.

Services for children

The Garden of Mothers and Children Centers are basically set up for two age groups. There are the 0-3 year olds who obviously come with a parent or with an older sister or a grandparent usually, and they stay with the child. Toys and equipment have been provided to cater to babies and smaller infants. For many parents the under 3s are seen as passive and dependent and in need of care and food, but not requiring a learning environment with objects, toys, and activities to stretch and develop their burgeoning curiosity and capabilities. Offering an inviting and informal space for adults and very young children to socialize has had a positive benefit for the mothers and for young children.

The other main age group are children aged 3-6 years old, and the focus here has been to develop their physical, intellectual, and socialization skills through activities based on play and experimenting with objects, mediums, and the environment. At first the children were over-awed and quiet by the variety of toys and opportunities given to them in the Centers. Children who had attended state nurseries were also amazed at the difference between the expectations of the staff and the methods employed in the two settings. State kindergartens still tend to rely on the older traditional methods of treating children as passive recipients and teaching by rote. Kindergarten classes can be dark, bare rooms with desks and chairs in lines, with children squashed together, and few resources to encourage children to develop enquiring minds.

What we offered, therefore, was very new and different to what the mothers and children were used to. The children loved it. The children particularly liked to use their hands and their imaginations engaging with dough, water, sand, paints, construction bricks, and junk art. Many parents at first did not appreciate their children playing, as they were unable to see how this would enable them to prepare for school and learn how to read and count. The Administrative Mothers and the volunteers have learned how to set up different types of activities within the room to accommodate the children's needs and interests. Counting, learning numbers, and the alphabet are part of the daily activities alongside nursery rhymes, storytelling, drawing, and writing. Children are eager to come to the Centers and to have the opportunities to see their friends and to play with the toys. For some of the children it represents an important break from the stresses within their homes related to the blood feuds.

We have provided ideas on how the Administrative Mothers and volunteers can use easily and readily available resources. As they are located in rural areas there is a wealth of natural substances (leaves, conkers, fir cones, and twigs) that they can use to make collages, models, or pictures. Some Centers have used dried pasta as a medium for pictures. For some of the Centers that have an outside area, large pieces of equipment have been bought so that the children can develop their gross motor skills and enjoy the clean mountain air.

Children in a traditional Albanian kindergarten.

Children and parents attending one of the Garden of Mothers and Children Centers in Albania.

Training and support for mothers

Alongside the activities for children, we have placed a big emphasis on trying to address some of the more fundamental problems outlined earlier in terms of the young mothers' social isolation and poor standing in the community, as well as their poor health and nutrition and general lack of awareness. While attending the Centers, the mothers have had both informal and much more formal training sessions. They have had sessions on the stages of child development from birth to six years old, the UN Convention on the Rights of the Child, the importance of play for children, creating a positive environment that stimulates the child's development and growth, nutrition, child immunization, and non-physical forms of discipline. This latter issue has been important as many parents still use physical and quite extreme corporal punishment to discipline their children. For example, a common saying told to me is "if you beat a child, then you love the child."

Health services are also provided to the children and mothers who attend the Centers. This includes information, training, and check-ups by a gynecologist, pediatrician, and family planning advisor. These services are much appreciated by the women who have little information about pregnancy, children's illnesses, and reproductive health. Due to the isolation of many of the women and children, the health service providers will also make monthly home visits to undertake check-ups, give advice, and/or refer them to other specialists.

Reaching out to the men and conflict resolution work

Interestingly, the Centers have also provided the opportunity to reach out to the men. We have, for example, run training sessions with the Fathers' Boards on children's rights and then look at child development, because men do not generally play a part in the care of young children. That is seen as very much the women's role. Men tend to take a little more interest when their child goes to formal education, but anything before that is not seen as needing their attention. We have, therefore, placed a big emphasis on raising people's awareness that it is very important to have a positive, calm, and stimulating environment for children, and that the men do have a very crucial role in the early education of children, in their development, and in their care.

One of the key things we have developed is a manual for fathers — "Roli I Baballareve Ne Mirerritjen e Femijeve" — which has had an amazing reception, from women as well as men, because there is nothing else that addresses the roles of fathers with their children. Whenever we have taken it to a conference or seminar and we have talked about it, it is the first publication to go. We have presented copies to the Minister of Education who has young children himself, and we are hoping that if we can begin to change prominent men's views about the importance of fathers to young children that we can over a period of time make a difference.

The manual is also about raising women's awareness that men can change a nappy, they can bathe a small child, they can play and care for their young daughter or son, and that they should be doing that. The manual covers everything — aspects of pregnancy, the changes in a woman's body, and how the woman feels. It also gives basic information on the baby's and child's development up to the age of six years. For example we looked at social development, play, language, physical and intellectual development, giving practical ideas of what fathers could do to encourage these areas of development through play and also to enable them to bond and develop a relationship with their child. I was able to provide some ideas for the youngest age groups as this is where the largest gap was.

One of my colleagues told me how one of her female friends had used the manual to encourage her husband to have more interaction with their child.

The friend had left the manual on the coffee table open to a certain page. Following reading the page, her husband bathed their child. This is one small example of where we have changed one man's outlook and improved his relationship with his child. Hopefully similar things have happened in other families. We have had some men take the books as well, so we think that they are interested to learn more.

Moreover, through this work with the Fathers' Boards, we have progressively been able to start addressing wider issues. One of these issues has been capacity building in terms of providing training to the Fathers' Boards so that they had the skills to advocate for preschool education for the children and their communities and to ensure that their Centers were sustainable. We approached this in several ways, including the provision of training on needs assessment, development of project proposals, budgeting, participatory assessments, fundraising, and project cycle management. In the last year we have progressed to the development and registration of two of the Fathers' Boards as NGOs, one in Peshkopi and the other in Kukes. The aim of this is to further the role of the men of the communities to seek ways of meeting the needs of young children by working with local government and donors through developing new services or improving what already exists.

As the presence of blood feuds and its effects on children was part of the originating project, we have also been able to start training and discussions on how to ameliorate and resolve some of the blood feuds with the Fathers' Boards. As mediators are used by families embroiled in conflict, some of the members of the Fathers' Boards as well respected members of their communities were well placed to act as mediators. Training was provided on mediation and conflict resolution techniques and how to avoid disagreements escalating into physical fights. Although the exact number of families and children involved in blood feuds in the four districts is not known, the impact on any family is immense. The

project has been evaluated by the National Albanian Center for Social Studies (NACSS) and the evaluators have stated that there had been 43 mediations between families and that the mediation had prevented any further violence.

Although this is a small number, it is significant given we have only been operating for two and a half years. I think that the only way blood feuds can be resolved or further violence can be prevented is through talking and discussion and also stronger and effective legal intervention. Part of the process set out in the Kanun is the role of the mediator. The action taken by members of the Fathers' Boards has demonstrated that this is an effective method of assisting families to halt the feuds. Albania has a lively café bar life in which people — primarily men — sit, drink coffee, and talk. It is the venue for many business discussions and allows for a less formal environment in which to discuss ideas and plans. I think that what has taken place in the Fathers' Boards has been a modification of the café discussions which has led to the discussion of issues including the blood feuds and early childhood education. The men of the communities are able to change how communities and individuals behave and this has been one venue for this to happen.

Personal reflections

Overall, our work in Albania has been really encouraging and we are seeing some important positive developments taking place. The mothers are commenting on how they have seen how their children are different. Many of them have said: "this son was born before I attended the Garden of Mothers and Children Centers and this son, he is a CCF baby, because I learned all about my pregnancy, the changes in my body, what to expect in labor and that I should talk to my baby, you know, from birth." The children are also noticeably much more confident when they come to the Centers; they relate well to their peers and are able to count and recite rhymes and sing songs.

Elementary school teachers have commented on the differences between children who have attended the Garden of Mothers and Children Centers and those who have either not attended a preschool or have attended a state kindergarten. They have reported that the children from our Centers have tended to be more enquiring and talkative and more able to make decisions and are eager to learn. The children also tend to know what to expect in the school setting. The activities and the methods that have been used in the Centers, therefore, aid their development and future education a great deal.

We should remember that in some of the Centers there are children attending whose families are caught up in blood feuds. For these children the Centers have been a welcoming, safe, and activity-based environment that has helped them deal with the anxiety and effects of death, fear, and the loss of a parent or family relative through the blood feuds. Young children are adaptable and resilient and many can deal with issues that adults find difficult. However, they need to have opportunities to be themselves and to develop their own interests and peer relationships.

In addition, the mothers are more confident. They have increased their knowledge and have a much wider level of awareness regarding health and children's needs and developmental issues. Increasing the women's knowledge of their own physical and biological functions and how to maintain and have a healthy lifestyle and home environment has improved the whole family's outlook. I cannot say that probably in many of the families we have changed everyone's attitudes or behaviour as it is a very gradual process at the individual family level, but it is a start.

Beyond this, however, I think our project demonstrates the potential role that early years' services can play in contributing to attitudes of non-violence and conflict resolution and promoting peace. Through focusing on the needs of children and families we have been able to gain the trust and

respect of the fathers, and because of this we have been able to begin exploring a range of issues with them, including the whole issue of mediation and conflict resolution. There is something about the early years that allows us to do this, whereas it may not be easy or possible via other avenues.

Lessons learned

In reflecting upon our experiences to date there are three main lessons I have learned through this project. First, there is a need to work with the men of the community. This was particularly relevant here in northern Albania which has a very patriarchal society. To get the Centers going, we had to put in a lot of work first in terms of working with the local government structures, the elders of the villages, the men, and the women. The way we organized the Centers basically reflected this with the need to establish Fathers' Boards to keep that initial engagement with those in decision making roles going.

The second lesson for me follows on from this first one and it's about working from where the local communities are at. At the outset, a key decision was taken not to try to change the patriarchal nature of the society in northern Albania but to work with it, in the initial stages at least. Personally, I was not too happy about working alongside traditional patriarchal lines as this supports the status quo; and if we are developing new ways of caring for children it would be an opportunity to also address issues of equality and rights for women. Looking back on it now, I think that it was right to work with the systems that were in place then. I think now that we have developed a level of trust and are accepted as an agency that works at the community level and listens to the people, it is probably the time to begin the work of bringing together the men and the women. Similar approaches of learning to respect another man and not to kill him or another member of his family, can be developed into learning to respect women and their role within society. This, then, is very much an area that we are now able to begin working on.

This, in turn, leads into the final key lesson for me to draw from our experience here and that is the need to locate the work within a clear community development philosophy that is about building understanding and awareness and also, crucially, the capacity of the local community to run the Centers themselves. As mentioned earlier, we have already been able to encourage two of the Fathers' Boards to register as NGOs in the hope that they would look at methods of fundraising and sustainability for some of the Centers. We also did some training with the Administrative Mothers on ways to fundraise at a local level by holding small events. Unfortunately, these ideas are unfamiliar and unprecedented in Albanian culture so more effort and assistance will be needed before we can truly say that the Garden of Mothers and Children Centers can be truly sustainable by the communities in which they are based.

Chapter Three

Bosnia and Herzegovina — Sarajevo: Radmila Rangelov-Jusović's Story

The war in Bosnia and Herzegovina has been identified as the most brutal conflict in Europe since World War II. Between 1992 and 1995 hundreds of thousands of people were caught up in the ensuing terror. The focus on "ethnic cleansing" led whole communities to be displaced or destroyed. Many people were incarcerated in concentration camps, tortured, and/or exterminated without due process of law. Sarajevo, and some other cities, were subject to daily bombings and sniper fire. Families in a number of remote villages and towns were subject to genocide.

The Center for Educational Initiatives Step by Step was established at the end of the war to promote democratic changes in the education system of Bosnia and Herzegovina. It has focused on creating safe spaces for children to develop and learn and for parents and educators to come together. Through its diverse training programs, the Center is playing an important role in helping to re-establish confidence and trust among local communities and thus build peace.

In this chapter Radmila Rangelov-Jusović tells the story of the development of the Center for Educational Initiatives Step by Step, the challenges it has faced, and the lessons learned from this. Radmila is the Executive Director of the Center. She was born in Sarajevo and grew up in a multiethnic and multireligious community typical in Bosnia during that time. Radmila's family mirrored this diversity: her father Bulgarian; her mother Serbian; her husband Muslim. During the war, Radmila's home was under siege. A bomb killed her father and severely wounded her mother, who died some years later. Her brother, his family, and many other close friends emigrated. Radmila chose to stay and work to help rebuild her country.

Bosnia y Herzegovina — Sarajevo: La historia de Radmila Rangelov-Jusović

Radmila Rangelov Jusović nació en Sarajevo y creció en una comunidad multiétnica y pluri-religiosa típica de Bosnia en aquella época. La familia de Radmila era un reflejo de esta diversidad: su padre era búlgaro, su madre serbia, y su esposo musulmán.

Durante la guerra el hogar de Radmila estuvo bajo el fuego. Una bomba mato a su padre e hirió severamente a su madre, quien murió algunos años después. Su hermano, su familia y muchos amigos cercanos emigraron. Radmila eligió quedarse y ayudar a reconstruir su país. Ella es ahora Directora Ejecutiva de una ONG local independiente: el Centro de Innovaciones Educativas Paso a Paso, establecido para promover cambios democráticos en el sistema educativo de Bosnia y Herzegovina.

The conflict in Bosnia and Herzegovina

Bosnia and Herzegovina is one of the six republics of the former Socialistic Federal Republic of Yugoslavia, with a population of approximately four million people and a long history of multiethnic and multireligious tradition. There are three primary ethnic groups in the region: Bosnian Muslims or Bosniacs (43 percent); Bosnian Serbs (31 percent), and Bosnian Croats (17 percent). Other groups from the area include Jews, Roma, and Albanians.

In 1992 three states of the former Yugoslavia declared independence: Slovenia; Croatia; and in March 1992, Bosnia and Herzegovina. As a result, war in Bosnia started. Hundreds of thousands of people were caught up in the ensuing terror. Whole communities were displaced or destroyed. Huge numbers of people (majority non-Serbs) were incarcerated in concentration camps, tortured, and/or exterminated without due process of law. Sarajevo, and some other cities, were subject to daily bombings and sniper fire. Families in a number of remote villages and towns were subject to genocide.

The International Criminal Tribunal has estimated that, across the country, victims of the war include over 55,000 civilians and over 47,000 soldiers. Moreover, it is estimated that over 20,000 women and girls are reported to have been raped. Massacres of whole villages have been reported. In one small, UN-protected area of Srebrenica, more then 8,000 Bosnian Muslims are reported to have been murdered. More than one million people were internally displaced and a further one million people became refugees in other countries. Within this, children account for more than 16,000 of those killed. In addition, over 34,000 children were severely wounded and more than 600,000 are estimated to be internally displaced; thousands more are living in refugee camps beyond the borders.

The war ended politically with the *Dayton Peace Agreement* signed in December 1995. Under the terms of this agreement, Bosnia and Herzegovina consist of two autonomous entities based on ethnicity. The first, Republika Srpska, covers 49 percent of the territory and represents a majority of ethnic Serbs. The remaining 51 percent became the Federation of Bosnia and Herzegovina and consists of ten administrative units each with its own legislature, executive, and judiciary branches (cantons). Each canton is populated by a majority of Bosniacs and/or Croats and has its own unique governmental structure, including individual Ministries of Education (13 in total). In order to make national policy, all 13 Ministries need to work in accord.

The effect of the conflict on children, families, and communities

The war in Bosnia and Herzegovina has been identified as the most brutal conflict in Europe since World War II. Every community has been affected. For years the basic essentials of survival — water and food — were scarce. There was no possibility of movement or travel. People remained hidden in their houses or in shelters. Since the war, the country remains covered with land mines. Some areas of the country remain "ethnically clean." Thousands of survivors reported that they could not face returning to villages where violence, rape, and killings had taken place. But in the end, many did return. As of September 2006, about one-half of the two million displaced are living in their home villages. However, finding the courage to return to a destroyed landscape and infrastructure is only one of many obstacles to overcome. There are limited or no jobs in the devastated environment to return to. As a result, more than 20 percent of people in Bosnia and Herzegovina currently live below the poverty line.

Children were victims of the war in myriad ways. Children lived under constant threat of violent death, either of themselves or of family members. Thousands of children were confined in basements or other enclosures. If not directly injured or killed, children became witnesses to the killing or rape of family members. Thousands became orphans, living in deep poverty. There was no consistent strategy for providing help to children. Children with physical injuries could not access proper medical care. The psychological needs of children who were variously traumatised, displaced, and/or injured were not addressed in any systemic way.

Post-war preschool and education services

At the end of the war the country remained with its original borders intact — but with a destroyed infrastructure, a destabilised economy, and a citizenry full of fear and mistrust. More than half of all the schools in the country were destroyed or became refugee camps, hospitals, and military facilities. To this day, the government has not returned all the preschools and schools that were seized for other purposes during the war, nor have they rebuilt the many school buildings that were destroyed.

One outcome of the conflict has been the establishment of three separate departments of education, with three separate curricula, standards, and programs (Serb, Croat, and Bosnian). Huge diversities exist in perspective, curriculum, and content provided by each system. For example the textbooks from different areas of the country present differing (often biased) geographical and historical facts related to the war. In the communities where one nationality is predominant, children are not taught about other national ethnicities. In areas where Croats and Bosniacs live in the same communities, the phenomenon of "two schools under one roof" has emerged. Children are educated in the same buildings, but each ethnic group attends in separate shifts. The children never mix socially and are not given opportunities to communicate with each other or even walk on the same side of the street.

The right of children to be educated in their mother tongue (cited in the *UN Convention on the Rights of the Child*) is used by politicians to support ethnic segregation in schools. This means that the limited resources allocated for education need to be spent on publishing textbooks in three languages (Bosnian, Serbian, and Croat). Prior to the war most children had fluency in all three languages from an early age.

Building trust relationships through early childhood education

A number of humanitarian aid agencies invested in Bosnia and Herzegovina after the war. Post-trauma and peace making programs were quickly set up, but the urgency of the situation and the perceived need for a quick response resulted in programs that were not always informed by situation analyses, or by local input. Many of the immediate post-war programs thus did not include a plan for systemic and sustainable development. It was within this climate that the *Center for Educational Initiatives Step by Step* developed.

The mission of the Center was, and still is, to provide quality education for all children. We are privileged in accessing stable funding sources which allows for a long-term vision. This gave us the opportunity to incorporate the building of trusting relationships as a critical component of educational planning and delivery. Trust needed to be rebuilt between teachers who now found themselves addressing ethnically different goals, and trust needed to be rebuilt with families and children who had learned to be suspicious and fearful of activities outside of the house. We needed to establish a new way of delivering preschool and educational services. We knew that community consultation and input would be the cornerstone of our success. Our efforts had to reflect trust of local expertise and build incrementally on local capacity.

Our first phase for reconstruction and development of the educational system concentrated on repairing buildings where preschools could be housed. This concrete act gave hope to communities. The buildings represented a commitment to permanence and stability within communities. The next phase was more complex. We needed to turn the physical classrooms into meeting places where all participants — children, families, and staff — felt welcomed, respected, and safe. This meant facilitating some radical changes in teaching attitudes and methods, including the notion that parents participate in classroom activities.

In our reconstructed system, teaching methods and curricula would be directed at promoting democracy within classrooms and hopefully beyond. Preschools and school would model respect for children's rights, freedom of speech and religion, and would teach children to think critically, make responsible choices and decisions, express themselves freely, and learn how to resolve conflict resolution in positive ways.

Working with and building the capacity of early childhood educators

Early childhood educators, like all citizens, had suffered during the war and needed to address their own physical and psycho-social needs. They, like so many, may have been unable to carry out their duties during the war and may have lost self-confidence along with the trust of the community. Most importantly, teachers needed to be models for forgiveness; to transcend their own biases and to reflect a positive outlook for the children in their charge. Educators also needed support in issues such as conflict resolution, problem solving, and respecting diversity.

In addition, early childhood educators in Bosnia and Herzegovina were unlikely to have had training in early childhood education. They were used to traditional didactic teaching methods. Thus, besides dealing with the needs of a reconstructed society,

teachers needed to feel comfortable working in a child-centered, integrated environment which called on significant parent involvement. Teachers also were expected to model problem solving techniques, teamwork, and respect for diversities.

This demanded huge change and placed a significant responsibility on the shoulders of early childhood teachers. Our first activity, therefore, was to call a national seminar for all appropriate teaching staff to begin the process of capacity building and forging support networks. Thus, only one year after the war, while the wounds were still fresh, we brought preschool teachers from different parts of the country and different nationalities together. I have to admit we took a risk here. The teachers came from warring factions. Besides needing to transcend their own differences, they also needed to learn how to work with parents in new inclusive ways and to challenge their own beliefs about how to teach young children. They needed to move from purveyors of information and knowledge to becoming facilitators of learning processes. It was going to be a huge jump for some — but in the end, the teachers embraced these activities and more!

An important component of the ultimate success of the teacher-training program was the opportunity for interactions and networking. The teachers, forced to spend time together during long breaks and evening events, got to know each other as individuals and to note their similarities as well as their differences. While we covered content based on child-centered learning, and while this was new and fascinating to some, it was the process more than the product which underlay our success.

We modeled participation in all ways. Learning took place through formal and informal discussion groups and the opportunity to share experiences and concerns. Teachers needed to regain their confidence by being treated as competent professionals; being listened to and being also supported to address issues in a way that was comfortable for them. Most of all it was important that they were seen as equal partners in determining the goals and focus of the training situation. This is the way we hoped the teachers would deal with their own constituency of parents and children.

Allowing participants to drive the training called for a great deal of flexibility on our part, including some radical changes in our original plans and refocusing on how to invest received funds. (Flexible donors are critical to success!) Often we found ourselves dealing with issues which were not obviously connected to promoting quality education systems, but were important to the teachers and, therefore, justifiable under our mandate.

In subsequent years we developed and presented a number of diverse training programs for all stakeholders. (See Boxes 3.1 and 3.2 for a sample of our programs.) While many training opportunities were presented, teachers reported that the most valued activity was the networking and the sharing of knowledge and experience amongst the groups. Many teachers visited each other in different cantons to share experiences and ideas. Through word of mouth, the trainings became hugely popular. When our funds were short, teachers found ways to raise money themselves and/or would spend several weeks' salary to attend.

Working with parents

One common outcome of war is that the trust between children and adults is often destroyed. Parents may disappear, causing children to feel deserted, neglected, and betrayed. Even when parents remain with the family during war situations, they often lose their ability to act as a source of protection or as the provider of basic needs. Because of this, a critically urgent task in post-conflict situations is to provide support for families to reunite and stabilize their relationships with their children.

Parents benefit from understanding how trauma may affect young children and from learning strategies to deal with this. Also, by facilitating healing for their children, parents themselves may actually be working

through their own psychosocial issues. In our program we worked hard to secure home/centre relationships. Parents, often traumatized themselves, needed to be given many ways in which they could participate. We worked with the educators to help them see the benefits of inviting parents to participate in classroom activities, to attend workshops and even, when possible, to work as salaried teacher's assistants.

The development of appropriate indicators for measuring success

Our mandate in establishing new preschools included a focus on measurable indicators and practice guidelines for use in early childhood settings. This need for accountability was new to us but became a basis for close collaboration with teachers. While conscious of the need to incorporate international standards for early childhood education, we were nonetheless committed to adapting any established programs to meet our specific needs. Early childhood educators, teachers, and representatives from educational authorities worked together to identify the main foci for the curriculum and for "best teaching practice" in light of individual situations (standards). While the implementation of an accountability dimension could seem threatening, the new approach was actually embraced by teachers who reported feelings of ownership and enhanced understanding of the goals and anticipated outcomes of their work.

These collaboratively developed standards remain the only quality standards in our country and continue to provide guidance for many other teachers who want to improve their practice. (See www.coi-stepbystep.ba/eng/standardi.html). Alongside the development of standards we also initiated a certification process for early childhood teachers. This involved the development of a group of certifiers who were trained specifically for

Box 3.1 Education for Social Justice training program

The *Education for Social Justice* program run by Step by Step facilitates the self-examination of attitudes toward diversity. Community members, health and social workers, teachers, and minority representatives engage in open dialogue and develop common ways to improve the life of every citizen in their community without judgment or accusation.

One such program focused on addressing the widespread discrimination against Roma children. It involved regional educational authorities, municipality, social services, health providers, school representatives, civil society (mostly Roma NGOs), and community members in developing a long-term strategy.

The process began with a meeting whereby stakeholders came together and had an opportunity to address their own biases. The next step was to investigate and hear stories about systemic oppression. The group then goes through a series of exercises to develop practical, step-by-step strategies

for dealing with the issues raised — including how to ensure that teachers and parents participate in solution-oriented programs for social justice.

One way to ensure commitment from the communities themselves was to provide only partial funding for the program. This means that the community needs to raise some funding. In the process of applying for local funds, the participants will be ensuring that goals and outcomes are stated in terms of local community needs.

As one of the participants explained:

"I became aware of my own prejudice and got the tools for an active fight against discrimination. I felt, at least for a moment, what discrimination, oppression, and aggression meant. I learned about the language of observation, language of interpretation, and the effects of labeling. Most importantly I learned that I do not want to be part of a 'silent majority.' It is hard to act, but possible. The worst thing is to not do anything!"

mentoring and undertaking the certification process. We did whatever we could to enhance the visibility of our newly trained teachers. This served the double goal of rewarding and motivating the teachers and also served to renew community respect for and trust in the education system. Thus we did not simply provide a "paper certificate" but rather a process which involved teacher-to-teacher support and the creation of a network of role models who were ready to experiment with new skills and competencies.

Nonetheless, since our program did not extend to all schools, some divisions appeared. Those who were not involved and were used to more traditional ways of working with children and families became suspicious of the new approach. The Step by Step teachers were criticized for "too much work for

nothing," "experimenting," and "not exercising discipline in the classroom." This was addressed in two ways. First, the network of teachers with shared values and goals supported and sustained the trained population. Group meetings were arranged as often as possible as a way to re-energize and re-motivate teachers who were feeling "attacked" by their non-participating peers.

Second, our attention to measurable indicators provided justification for our methods. As time passed, the obvious benefits for the children and some international recognition allowed us to expand throughout the country. Original participating teachers became mentors and trainers to new recruits into the program. This raised their status in their communities and beyond.

Box 3.2 Parenting with Confidence program

The *Parenting with Confidence* program run by Step by Step aims to provide parents with information and strategies to work with their own children in lieu of preschool participation. The program involves the facilitation of peer support groups. Materials and workshops are included as a way to keep parents motivated. Topics include positive interactions with children, appropriate guidance techniques, building children's self-confidence, positive communication, and creating opportunities for children to develop literacy and numeracy skills within a relaxed home environment. Resources such as books and toys are provided.

The program is delivered by teachers within the community who have been given special training for this purpose. Space for meetings is usually arranged within schools or preschools. Often the parents (who tend to come from marginalized and disadvantaged populations) bring their children with them to the

"classes." This gives us an opportunity to undertake some pseudo preschool activities which the parents can observe and replicate at home. The program has been extremely popular and we are pleased to see that fathers are also taking part.

The confidence this gave parents is evident in some of the testimonies they provided:

"I was so afraid about my child starting the school. Now it is easier because the teacher told me that she doesn't have to know all the letters and numbers . . . and it's OK to color across the line. . . ."

"I realized that every child needs a time to learn. It takes time. . . ."

"Now I know how play is important, that a child is learning numbers and letters through play."

Box 3.3 Encouraging relationships with parents: The Children's Museum

One of our most successful activities for home and center collaboration was the development within our classrooms of a *Children's Museum*. This involved a contribution by each family for the collection of an item that should reflect some aspect of family life (baby pictures, clothes, something from a previous village) which the child and parent present to the class — including designing activities around their

item. The parent and child would answer questions about the item and then, ceremoniously, donate it to the museum. This activity allowed children and parents to talk about positive aspects of their past in a safe and supportive environment and provided the means for families to reconstruct a history based on pride and positive feelings.

Our program started in seven kindergartens. Today, professional development is available to every teacher in every village of Bosnia and Herzegovina. Instead of training the Step by Step teachers ourselves, we evolved into trainers of trainers. Currently, we have a network of 120 certified trainers who work with more than 1,000 teachers a year in local communities.

Lessons learned

In retrospect, our success lay in many things including providing a long-term vision for the future, remaining apolitical, and treating everyone equally without judgment. However, it mostly lay in simply listening and being willing to adapt processes to the needs of the local population. There are three key lessons we have learned from our experience to date:

Local ownership is vital

We believe that a big part of our success lies in our commitment to including all voices as we approached the development of new ideas and new programs. Sustainable change has come about through shared vision, values, beliefs, and ownership. We are convinced that the best programs in the world will not take hold without some adjustment to local needs, attitudes, and capacities. My advice is to: remain open and flexible; practice listening to all stakeholders; and allow for the time to implement change in incremental stages.

Change is based on developing trust relationships

The physical development of preschool spaces came to represent a metaphor for feelings of safety. Here all stakeholders could feel welcomed, comfortable, and could participate equally. Trust developed because we truly respected the commitment, experience, knowledge, and capacities of parents, teachers, and children. The time and effort taken to develop these safe and trusting spaces was well worth it. Only from this position could the overarching goals for educational and social change that we had set for ourselves be achieved.

Box 3.4   Views on the Step by Step programs

"Kindergartens and schools were the only facilities in communities and we tried to use them as a meeting place where life can begin to recover."
Early childhood teacher at training session

"Teachers and parents, when organized and supported, are always the biggest and strongest force for peace and reconciliation. They are also an extremely, very sensitive, and critical audience."
Trainer in Step by Step program

Co-opting diverse stakeholders will ensure sustained outcomes

Our strategy from the start was to collaborate with all of our stakeholders. This included the local governments of all 10 cantons, Republika Srpska, and District Brcko. We developed long-term partnerships with the 12 Ministries of Education (13 including the Federal Ministry). We included officially appointed representatives of all the Ministries as project coordinators. They became part of writing project proposals, standards development, and they participated in the trainings. It took several years of involvement to build up feelings of ownership. Today they have become advocates for changes within the system in every area.

Bosnia and Herzegovina has a long way to go to heal from the devastation of war. The children in our centres are still facing life within a deeply divided society. There are wounds which will take generations to heal. And yet, the success of the Step by Step project gives up hope. Teachers are feeling empowered. Parents are feeling included. Children are developing awareness of how to live and work and play in settings which are participatory and equitable. It is a first step.

Chapter Four

Chad:
Félicien Ntakiyimana's Story

Chad's post-independence history has been marked by civil war. From 1965 until the late 1980s, foreign troops have intervened in Chad's civil war to support one side against another (France, Libya, and the United States) or as part of an expansionist plan (Libya). During this period, national resources were used for military purposes with little or no investment in social and health services, with the inevitable result that poverty increased dramatically. Within this unstable security context, donors and international organisations have been reluctant to invest in Chad. The situation has therefore become an "overlooked crisis." The recent conflict in Western Sudan in the Darfur region resulted in a flow of more than 200,000 Sudanese refugees into Eastern Chad, exacerbating the already critical situation for families in the area.

In response, UNHCR (United Nations High Commissioner for Refugees) and its partners mounted a major logistics operation to establish refugee camps in some of the most desolate terrains on earth for thousands of people. Family shelters, latrines, clinics, schools, wells, and other infrastructure were literally built from the ground up. The first of these self constructed campsites opened in January 2004. These camps have created their own problems, however, not least in relation to tensions and conflict between refugees in the camps and those living in local villages.

In this chapter, Félicien Ntakiyimana relates the story of attempts to create safe environments for children in the midst of this turmoil and uncertainty. In discussing his recent experience working within the camps for UNICEF Chad as a United Nations Volunteer Program Officer in charge of child protection, Félicien highlights the role of child-friendly spaces and local community involvement in early childhood care and development. Félicien has extensive experience working in emergency situations. Before working in Chad, he worked as a foster care coordinator for CARE Australia in Katale Refugee Camp (Democratic Republic of Congo) and then as a social worker in charge of family tracing and fostering for UNICEF/Rwanda Emergency Operations in Goma.

Chad: La historia de Félicien Ntakiyimana

La historia post-independencia de Chad ha estado marcada por inestabilidad y violencia que surgen principalmente de tensiones entre un norte árabe musulmán, y un sur principalmente animista y cristiano. Desde 1965 hasta el final de la década de los 80, tropas extranjeras intervinieron en la guerra civil para apoyar a uno u otro lado en contra del contrario (Francia, Libia, y los Estados unidos) o como parte de sus planes expansionistas (Libia).

Durante este periodo, los recursos naturales fueron objetivo militar, y no hubo o fue muy escasa la inversión en servicios sociales y de salud. La pobreza se incremento dramáticamente. En este contexto de inestable seguridad, los donantes y las organizaciones internacionales han estado poco dispuestos a invertir en Chad. La situación se ha convertido en una "crisis no tenida en cuenta."

El conflicto reciente en Sudan occidental en la región de Darfur, ha causado la huida de mas de 200.000 sudaneses que se han refugiado en Chad occidental, exacerbando la situación de crisis ya existente para las familias de esta área. Sin embargo, la situación de crisis generada por los refugiados sirvió para enfocar la atención en Chad, y para canalizar algunos recursos hacia el país.

En este capitulo, Feliciten Ntakiyimana relata la historia de los intentos por crear ambientes seguros para los niños y niñas en medio de la turbulencia y la incertidumbre. Al discutir su reciente experiencia con el Programa de UNICEF en Chad como el Oficial del Programa de Voluntarios de las Naciones Unidas a cargo de de la protección de la infancia, Ntakiyimana resalta el papel de los espacios amigos de los niños y del involucramiento de la comunidad local en el cuidado y el desarrollo infantil temprano.

Background

The Republic of Chad is a landlocked country located in North Central Africa. The population of 10 million incorporates 200 distinct groups, speaking over 120 different languages or dialects. The three main religions are Islam (51 percent), Christianity (35 percent), and Animism (7 percent). The economy is primarily agricultural. Over 80 percent of Chad's population relies on subsistence farming and livestock raising for its livelihood. Chad is the fifth poorest nation in the world.

Life expectancy at birth in Chad is estimated to be 48 years. Approximately half of the population is under 14 years of age, with children 0-8 years of age accounting for 25 percent (about 2.5 million children). Infant mortality rates are among the highest in the world. An estimated 11,000 children are living on streets or in other oppressive circumstances which belie the Convention on the Rights of the Child (ratified by Chad in 1989). Thousands of nomadic children do not have access to any form of primary education. For thousands of other children, facilities are non-existent or in bad repair. Child care facilities are not available to the majority of the population. Most children of preschool age are cared for by their mothers or other family members who are likely to be

experiencing the deprivations of poverty. The majority of adults (especially mothers) are illiterate. Child trafficking, child prostitution, child marriage, and genital mutilation are common. Polygamy compounds the precarious situation of children and women (ECPAT, 2006).

The nature of the conflict

Chad has been enduring civil warfare amidst political and social disturbances since the 1970s, with concomitant displacement of populations, destruction of infrastructure, insecurity, and increasing pauperization of the local population. The country attained full independence from France on August 11, 1960, with Ngarta Tombalbaye as first president. Tombalbaye steadily strengthened his control over the country and by 1965, it had become a one-party state. In 1966, discontent among northern Muslim tribes with President Tombalbaye — a Christian southerner — developed into a full-scale guerrilla war. French troops helped battle the revolt, which ended in 1973. This undermined his rule and, in 1975, President Tombalbaye was killed in a coup led by Noël Milarew Odingar, who immediately passed power to yet another southerner, General Felix Malloum. Malloum also failed to end the war, notwithstanding his cooperation as Prime Minister in

1978 of the insurgent leader, Hissène Habré, head of the Armed Forces of the North (FAN). In 1979 Malloum was replaced by a Libya-backed northerner, Goukouni Oueddei. This precipitated the most anarchic phase of the Chadian Civil War.

Throughout the 1970s and 1980s, Libya had occupied various parts of Chad and supplied the Chad National Liberation Front (FROLINAT) with arms. Libya invaded Chad in 1980 to help Oueddei remain in power and to forward an expansionist policy with the goal of politically unifying Libya and Chad. France and the United States responded by aiding Habré in an attempt to contain Libya's regional ambitions. Civil war deepened. In 1980, Libya occupied all of northern Chad, but Habré defeated Libyan troops and drove them out in November 1981. By this stage, France and neighbouring Libya were intervening repeatedly to support one side against another. In 1982, Habré conquered the capital, ousted President Oueddei, and assumed overall control of the state. His eight year rein led to immense political turmoil. Human rights organisations accused Habré of ordering the execution of thousands of political opponents and members of tribes thought hostile to his regime.

In 1983, the Libyan troops occupied all the country north of Koro Toro. With the aid of France and the USA, Habré continued to fight Libyan occupation and defeated Qaddafi in 1987. Libya moved out of Northern Chad, with the exception of the Aouzou Strip and parts of Tibesti. In 1994, the International Court of Justice rejected Libya's claims and returned these areas to Chad. Despite his victory, Habré's government was weak, accused of brutality and corruption, and seemingly disliked by a majority of Chadians. Habré was deposed by Libyan-supported rebel leader Idriss Deby on December 1, 1990. A semblance of peace was restored. A democratic constitution was drafted and Presidential elections were held in 1996 and 2001.

Refugees arrive in eastern Chad

While the country was still struggling to overcome its own conflicts, the war in neighbouring Sudan affected Eastern Chad. Since February 2003, Western Darfur in Sudan experienced one of the fiercest manslaughters with the Janjaweed (militia) forcing over 200,000 people into exile in Eastern Chad. Almost two million more escaped to camps in Western Darfur. The refugees from Sudan who flowed into the remote desert region of Eastern Chad, arrived in an area already marked by scarce water and fuel wood resources. Makeshift shelters were constructed just metres from the frontier. These camps were dangerously isolated during the rainy season and were subject to cross-border raids by marauding militia. Treacherous and dangerous conditions meant that aid deliveries were nearly impossible.

In response, a major logistics operation was mounted in order to move the majority of the refugees to camps at a safer distance from the volatile border. In some of the most desolate terrains on earth, UNHCR and its partners constructed small villages for thousands of people. Family shelters, latrines, clinics, schools, wells, and other infrastructure were literally built from the ground up. The first of these self constructed campsites opened in January 2004. By September, a total of 10 camps had been established. Emergency airlifts flew in thousands of metric tons of tents, blankets, plastic sheeting, soap, and other relief items. However, the response to the refugee crisis by the international community had been very slow. By late 2004, ten camps had been established within the semi-desert, impoverished region. Water, fuel wood, and food remained endemically scarce.

When the humanitarian aid did arrive, it became a source of tension and conflict. The refugees had been depleting the scarce resources of the local population and now only they were deemed eligible for aid and supplies. The refugees became relatively well resourced compared to their national "hosts." This created growing resentment and hostility. Tensions between the refugee population and locals were exacerbated by the fact that the humanitarian workers in the camps were mostly recruited from outside the country or from south Chad. These workers earned salaries much greater than those of the local civil servants and teachers.

As disparities increased, the refugee camps and humanitarian workers became the target of conflict and violence. In 2005, new rebel groups emerged in western Sudan and have made attacks into eastern Chad, in central Chad, and in the capital city, N'djamena. In June 2005, President Idriss Deby removed constitutional provisions limiting the number of terms he could run. He was re-elected in May 2006. In June 2006, Chad complained to the UN Security Council that Sudan was backing armed groups who were carrying out raids in eastern Chad. At the time of this writing, the fighting across the borders continues.

The situation for children

At the time of the Darfur crisis, child protection needs in Chad included attention to child trafficking and prostitution, widespread child labour and exploitation, juvenile justice reform, social and economic reintegration for homeless and street children, and a dearth of psychosocial supports for children of all ages. However, the refugee cohort brought a new set of needs. Long-term conflict and deprivation and the recent atrocities experienced in Sudan had created a population of injured, sick, and severely traumatised children. Large numbers of children reported having lost their families and/or having seen friends killed or taken away. The majority had psychosocial disturbances which were manifested in nightmares and/or terror at daily occurrences such as the sound of a plane overhead. Most children did not feel safe in the camps and believed that an attack was imminent. Over 35 percent of the refugees exhibited signs of acute malnutrition (U.S. Center for Disease Control and

Prevention, 2004). These children arrived into overcrowded and under resourced camps, often situated in areas polluted with land mines.

Several categories of children were shown to be particularly vulnerable in terms of safety, wellbeing, and access to support and services. These included children with disabilities, young boys who could be forced into army service, and girls of all ages at risk of rape. Separated and unaccompanied children were shown to be the most vulnerable to sexual and physical abuse and the least likely to have access to available camp services (CCF Chad, 2006).

Programs to address children's needs

When I arrived in Chad in 2004, the situation for the thousands of refugee children was as bad as anything I had ever seen. The Darfur crisis was gaining momentum, bringing thousands of children into a region already deprived of infrastructure and resources. During the briefing sessions I was given on arrival, I found many reasons to leave the country as soon as possible. The security situation was extremely volatile. I was advised never to walk in the streets and to take up security guards for my residence. I left immediately to visit the refugee camps in eastern Chad. What I witnessed there was beyond anything I had ever seen or imagined.

The region was semi-desert, with scarce water, food, and fuel wood resources. There was endemic malnutrition among the children. There were no recreational facilities or equipment. Some children had been so traumatized by bombings in their Darfur region that when a helicopter or a plane passed by, they screamed and sought hiding. As I had seen elsewhere, the refugee crisis in Eastern Chad was so huge, so problematic and, in many ways, so political, that the children — the silent victims — tended to be of little or no priority. When I left the camps to return to N'djamena, I was exhausted; but there was no question about my next directions. Perhaps I had survived the Rwandan prisons in order to help other people overcome hardships and despair. I had decided to stay on.

The initial need for the children was obvious: they needed to survive. Thus, one of the priorities was to address the chronic malnutrition. After this we needed to ensure an environment of predictability and normalcy so that psychosocial healing could begin. There was also a desperate need for programs to support parents and caregivers. At the same time, we were conscious of the need to build in sustainable programs, so that outside intervention could be minimised as soon as possible.

These needs were addressed in three major programs:

- The establishment of therapeutic feeding centres and child friendly spaces
- The recruitment and training of Animators (unsalaried volunteers with no certified qualifications) from within the refugee community
- The establishment of child protection committees

Each of these programs had spin off outcomes which went beyond original emergency interventions. In the sections following I describe some of our projects and outcomes. This represents only a small part of the historical and complex story of Chad and Sudanese refugees. It is a snapshot of conflict and desperate conditions, which at the time of writing still seem to be unending. Nonetheless, there is no doubt in my mind that the programs for young children which somehow got established in refugee camps and surrounding communities had, and continue to have, long-term outcomes. Beyond crisis intervention, the early childhood programs provided vehicles for addressing social justice, enhancing gender equity, and empowering communities. Despite the horrendous conditions then and now, this is my story about hope.

Therapeutic feeding centres and child-friendly spaces

The main strategy for dealing with malnourished and traumatised children was to support the establishment of therapeutic feeding centres where anti-starvation diets were distributed. Starving children mostly do not have the energy or desire to eat. For this reason food is given in small amounts, throughout the day. In the tents, food distribution took place at 7 a.m. and 3 p.m. Most families had nowhere to go in between these feedings. They simply sat around and waited. In response, it was decided to support a program of child-friendly spaces attached to or close by feeding centres around Iridimi, Kounoungo, Touloum, and Mile refugee camps.

Child-friendly spaces are physical areas where children and their caregivers can feel safe and take part in structured and unstructured activities. The spaces are mainly aimed at children from ages 0-15 years, although adult programs are also available. Our child-friendly spaces served many purposes:

- They provided an oasis where children and family members could feel safe and relaxed.
- They kept children active and engaged in their environment during the long wait between feedings.
- They offered both free play activities and structured events to help counter trauma in children.
- They addressed the needs of mothers and caregivers. Classes and training were offered for adults on topics such as literacy, early childhood development, and income generation.
- They provided a place for distressed adults to discuss their issues and share their concerns.
- Since children could attend on their own, use of these spaces provided respite time for parents and caregivers and gave them opportunities to attend to chores and other activities.

The use of community Animators

The child-friendly centres were staffed by Animators, recruited from within the community. Most Animators were unsalaried volunteers with no certified qualifications. It was felt that the ability to communicate with the children and families, to reflect familiar habits and mores, and to model a calm outlook were more important traits for Animators than having had formal training in a far different context. The main task of the Animators was to develop recreational and other activities for all children within a relaxed and "normalised" atmosphere. Animators received a training program which focussed on creating structured, predictable, and healing environments for traumatised children. The use of refugees as staff members had benefits beyond the program for children. Becoming an Animator represented a taking back of control over their own lives and a regaining of their self-image as competent caretakers for their children. Animators also provided positive role models for the children as capable, active adults with whom they could relate. In this way opportunities were opened up for the post-trauma effects of both the adults and the children to begin to be addressed.

Emergency situations can give rise to changed social conditions. In Chad, necessity and shortages resulted in the recruitment of both male and female Animators, working together. The teams represented a previously taboo situation in this Muslim region/community where gender segregation for workers had been the norm. Similarly, children in the child-friendly spaces, and subsequently in schools which were developed, were not segregated by gender.

Box 4.1   Child-friendly spaces in the Chadian refugee camps

The children in the camps have lost their homes, friends, schools, and sometimes their families. Child-friendly spaces provide psychosocial support to children and adolescents, stimulating their learning and well-being in a protective environment. Activities range from sports to learning about hygiene to parental sensitization. Also they give children access to adults other than their parents, who are likely to be suffering from trauma themselves. Staff are trained to observe children for post-traumatic stress disorder — and to refer any showing the signs to medical partners for counseling. There's trust here, people to trust. And they gain confidence.

As Masumbuko (2005) has explained: "The most vulnerable children are those in therapeutic or supplementary feeding. Emaciated children have no appetite. They just want to sit or lie with their mother. But children learn from each other. Seeing another child sit upright, they will start to sit upright.

Then they say, "If they can run, why can't I run?" When they start being interested in playing, they also get an appetite.

"The effects of child-friendly spaces are visible in many other ways. At first the children were drawing helicopters, guns, blood, violence, men on horses, houses on fire, bombs, and people with one leg — every type of violence you can imagine, including sexual violence against women and girls. This they brought out in their drawings. Now this is beginning to change; they are drawing nature, flowers, donkeys, rivers, beautiful faces, and classrooms. The child-friendly spaces have begun to change the way the children look at things."

I've seen children arrive at the child-friendly spaces seeming really afraid, and then becoming much more relaxed. There's a big change. Now the children smile, they're happy, they play.

In September 2004, I visited a class in Kounoungo refugee camp where Animators were being trained. My first impression was that both male and female future Animators were happy to work together, regardless of sexual biases. I asked just one question to the males — whether they were at ease being trained by women (the trainers were women from the Chad Ministry of Social and Family Affairs). They told me that they understood that women were equal to men and that both sexes needed to contribute to the welfare of children!

Another special aspect was that female children attended the programs to the same extent as male children. Acceptance of this notion was helped by the fact that girls were not needed for household activities, since there were not many domestic chores which could be attended to in the camps. On my visit to a Farchana refugee camp, I met the Headmaster of a school and discussed the activities of his school. While I was still there, I saw a number of women running into classrooms after the children had gone home. The Headmaster told me that those were illiterate women who had decided to use the classes in the afternoons for literacy and numeracy activities. I also talked to a female teacher. She told me that she felt at ease working with her male colleagues, and that this would have been extremely difficult, if not impossible, in Sudan.

Grassroots responsibility: Child Protection Committees (CPCs)

In our search for sustainable programs we facilitated the development of child protection committees (CPCs). All CPC members were from the refugee community. If needed, assistance and guidance from host country social workers was available. The child protection committees were established to assess and monitor children's rights within the camps. CPCs oversaw the child-friendly spaces. They made local and thus relevant decisions about locations of spaces, access to spaces, and which programs would be

developed. CPCs also had an advocacy role and organised awareness raising for refugee families and other decision makers about needs and rights of children.

Once again, the emergency situation resulted in a progressive approach to child protection. Under normal circumstances within Sudan, the CPCs (if they existed at all) would have remained in the hands of bureaucrats and professionals. In the camps, grass roots individuals, mothers, fathers, and others were mobilised in their quest to ensure that conditions for their children were as health promoting (and as equitable) as possible. The CPC volunteers received information, training, and support. This was unlikely to have been available in their homeland.

There were a number of unintended consequences of these programs. Increased attention to the plight of children in the camps inevitably resulted in attention being given to children in the local areas surrounding the camps. The need to extend the child protection program to children in the villages as well as those within the camps became apparent to all.

However, the needs of local children were very different from those of the refugee population. An intervention could not simply be extended from one situation to the other. After intensive assessments, three main elements for child protection were identified for the Chadian children. There were: 1) legal and legislative reforms, 2) social integration, and 3) mine-risk education. Thus, the refugee crisis in eastern Chad prompted progressive attention to and discussion on legislative reforms and on the situation of children in eastern Chad, which may not have otherwise been addressed. These included the situation of children in institutions, such as the Koran-memorizing centre of Dar-as-Salaam in Abéché.

At the central government level, new draft bills were prepared to reform the penal and labour codes, outlawing the worst forms of child labour; a national policy on orphans and other vulnerable children, including those affected/infected by HIV/AIDS, was developed; and national policy for the protection of children against sexual abuse and commercial exploitation was drafted. A study on the situation of children working as domestic aides was carried out. A number of other steps at the macro and policy level were also instigated. These included the development of national policy for early care and education, discussions around the development of a civil code, and attention to programs aimed at curbing violence in schools.

Another focus for Chadians targeted skills training and/or school reintegration for large cohorts of children who fell between the cracks of other programs. This included street children, child prostitutes, children in forced labour, children in institutions, detention centres, and in suspicious "religious training" centres. As such, a long overdue program for birth registration was initiated. At the time, less than 25 percent of children born in Chad were registered. The UN facilitated sensitization campaigns about this issue and developed birth registration materials which were widely disseminated.

Mine-risk education also became a new priority. A program was developed to integrate mine risk awareness into the school curricula. This was particularly important for the highly polluted east Chad region. Finally, a system of Garderie Communautaire (Social Care Centres) — similar to the child-friendly spaces of the refugee camps — was developed. This concept was developed with the assistance of the Government of Québec, Canada, in collaboration with UNICEF. An organizational and pedagogical guide for the Garderies has been written especially for Chad.

Box 4.2   Garderie Communautaire (Social Care Centres): A community-managed low-resource program for 3-6 year olds

Inspired from traditional practices, Garderie centers require minimal equipment. A group of 15 children aged between 3 and 6 years are cared for by three voluntary mothers on a rotation basis. The mothers form a kind of association that aims at taking care of the children of a village, especially the children from vulnerable households. The mothers receive training related to health, nutrition, and child development. They work under the supervision of a trained Animator. These centres are eligible to receive support and assistance from Ministry social workers, especially for technical assistance and for training local Animators, but are managed by communities themselves (Republic of Chad, Ministry of Social and Family Affairs, 2004).

Conclusions and lessons learned

The programs which were developed in the refugee camps of eastern Chad exemplify what can be done quickly, without trained staff or major resource support. The development of therapeutic feeding centres, child-friendly spaces, and child protection committees call upon organisational skills more than the need for resource deployment. Programs which ensure devolution of decision making to local grass roots agents and which model male/female integration and equity have long-term community development outcomes.

The refugee crisis created raised awareness for children's needs throughout Chad. The international aid agencies and the Ministry of Social and Family Affairs turned their focus onto sustainable support programs. The positive outcomes from the refugee programs have become a model for internal and international social developments. Thousands of children and their families living in Chad have been subject to the trauma of displacement, starvation, illness, violence, and continued conflict and hostility. There are no easy or quick fixes for their situation, but early childhood programs are helping.

The importance of child-friendly spaces

Child-friendly spaces can be established in the middle of difficult and hostile environments and can be organised and run with minimal resources. In the refugee camps in eastern Chad, members of the local community were given training and became responsible for ensuring a peaceful atmosphere in the designated spaces, despite conflict and danger close by. Children and adults understood that this was a judgment-free space where the only goal was to allow children to play and take part in activities in as normal a fashion as possible. The need to recruit from a small pool of eligible staff meant that some long-standing traditions were ignored. The use of both male and female Animators in the child-friendly spaces and the integration of girls and boys for play sessions represented a step towards greater social equity for females in Chad.

Crises can bring raised awareness

When the refugee situation within eastern Chad hit the western media and humanitarian aid began to flow in, the conditions of the general population simultaneously came to the attention of international aid agencies. The Darfur crisis prompted a focus on the need for systemic, sustainable child protection throughout Chad. While many oppressive conditions remain, there are now articulated goals and a number of programs in place to address endemic needs.

Communities heal when they have opportunities to help themselves

Some of the most challenging post-conflict obstacles are the feelings of depression, pessimism, and powerlessness in adults. Children cannot heal when those around them reflect despair. Programs which are designed, organised, and implemented by the target populations themselves serve two important goals: They ensure that programs are relevant and appropriate to the community and they empower the community to take charge. The sense of being in control of one's environment and the ability to enact improvements are powerful healing processes. In this way, the development of early childhood programs in the midst of difficult and oppressive situations is a potent enabler of hope.

The needs of children extend beyond the conflict period

Often it is when the violence has stopped that repressed trauma emerges. The situation for children and families who return to their homeland after a refugee experience is often characterised by a lack of infrastructure, deprivations, hardships, and other factors which contribute to fear, paranoia, and trauma. On return, adults may have difficulty transcending their resentment and biases. There is a danger that these will, wittingly or not, be transferred onto the young children in post-conflict situations. The need for committed and qualified social workers and psychologists may be strongest at this time, but it is often when the humanitarian support stops. In order to build/rebuild local capacity, psychosocial support should be included in any human resource development plans for conflict affected areas.

Chapter Five

Colombia:
Marta Arango's Story

For over 30 years, conflict and violence have permeated the nation of Colombia. Thousands of children of almost three generations have suffered from the death or displacement of family members; from the fear and terror of kidnapping; from poverty, illness, and lack of schooling; and, in many cases, from early deaths.

In 1976 Marta Arango and her husband Glen Nimnicht founded CINDE (Centro Internacional de Educación y Desarrollo Humano). CINDE's mission was to support the physical and psychological well being of young Colombians. As the effects of long-term violence on children became increasingly apparent, CINDE enhanced its goals and programs.

Currently CINDE runs community-centered programs for peace building and is a major player in the development of regional and national networks to serve children. Most uniquely, CINDE has developed collaborative graduate programs with universities as a way to ensure the development of specialists and leaders committed to the problems of children and youth. To date, more than 2,000 graduates have completed high-level degrees in this area.

In this chapter Marta Arango, Alejandro Acosta, and Milena Jaramillo tell the story of CINDE and its programs for peace within one of the most beautiful, and yet one of the most conflict-ridden and violent, nations in the world.

Colombia: La historia de Marto Arango
Centro Internacional de Educación y Desarrollo Humano

Por más de 30 años, el conflicto y la violencia han permeado la nación Colombiana. Miles de niños y niñas, de casi tres generaciones, han sufrido la muerte o el desplazamiento de miembros de su familia, el miedo y el terror del secuestro, la pobreza, enfermedades, falta de escolarización, y en muchos casos muerte temprana.

En 1976 Marta Arango y su esposo Glen Nimnicht fundaron CINDE — Centro Internacional de Educación y Desarrollo Humano. La misión de CINDE era apoyar el bienestar psicológico y físico de los colombianos jóvenes. A medida que los efectos de la violencia de largo plazo se hicieron evidentes, CINDE fortaleció sus metas y sus programas. Actualmente CINDE lleva a cabo programas para la construcción de paz basados en la comunidad y es un actor importante en el desarrollo de redes nacionales y regionales para beneficio de la niñez. De manera particular CINDE ha estado desarrollando programas de postgrado en convenio con universidades como una forma para asegurar el desarrollo de líderes y especialistas comprometidos con el desarrollo de la niñez y la juventud. Hasta la fecha más de 2000

profesionales se han graduado de estos programas.

Marta Arango, Alejandro Acosta y Milena Jaramillo cuentan la historia de CINDE y sus programas para la paz, en uno de los países mas bellos, y aun así mas violentos y conflictuados del mundo.

Background

Colombia is a land of infinite richness and biodiversity. Its beauty is reflected in lush jungle and forests, beautiful coasts, large plains, and rich fauna and flora. Colombians themselves are diverse and colorful. Colombian nationals are made up of Black, Amerindian, Caucasian, and mixed races. Colombia should be a paradise on earth. But underlying the beauty, there is a tragic tradition of armed conflict and destruction.

Colombia is one of the most violent countries in the world (Rubio, 97). Nearly every family in Colombia has been exposed in some way to the threat of kidnappings, extortion, and massacres. In the cities, protection gangs often have control of various areas, including roadways into the cities. In the country, rural homes and agricultural areas are threatened by unregulated mining, environmental destruction, and drug wars. Colombian citizens are three times more likely to die from homicides than they are from infectious or parasitic diseases and twice as likely to die from violence as from cardio-vascular problems (National Health Institute — Instituto Nacional de Salud, 1994). Kidnappings, landmines, environmental destruction, extreme rates of male mortality, and the long-term effects of displacement color the experience and the potential of each child.

In relation to kidnapping for ransom or revenge, this is a common characteristic of the Colombian scene: more than 15,000 people were kidnapped between 1999 and 2003; over 4,000 died in captivity. Hundreds

of kidnap victims are children (PCS y CNR, 2004). Kidnapping results in terror, trauma, psychological breakdown, destruction of families, and poverty. Living conditions can change drastically. Whole extended families become bankrupt from paying ransoms. When families cannot pay, victims are killed. Given that they are often the main breadwinners for their families, this leaves families without an income source.

As for land mines, they have been placed in nearly every area of the country, including cultivated fields, trails, areas near small towns and villages, and schools (Santos, 2003). Between 1990 and 2002, close to 2,000 land mine accidents, in over 400 different towns and areas, were reported. Children are often victims of landmine maiming or death.

Insurgent forces in Colombia have taken control of large tracts of land in jungle areas which are vital to the global ecosystem. These are good hiding places with extremely difficult access for outsiders. Rain forests have been destroyed and illegal cultivations have been developed. In an effort to weaken the economic base of the insurgents, the government of Colombia has adopted strategies such as massive fumigation — but this solution brings enhanced ecological consequences.

Insurgents have also taken over production zones which affect the national economy: gold mines in northeast Antioquia and southern Bolivar, oil in Arauca, bananas in Urabáj, and coal mines in Cesar and Guajira have been appropriated — cutting off large sections of the population from the benefits of these economies. Meanwhile, fighting and anarchy have affected the ecosystem. Violence and attacks have been blamed for the spilling of 2.3 million barrels of oil in Colombia. This amount is equivalent to 11 times that spilled in what was called the greatest ecological disaster in world history: that of the Exxon tanker (Rangel, 2004).

The impact of conflict on families and communities

The violence has had a number of effects on families and communities. Men are most vulnerable to the violence within Colombia. The tendency for family breadwinners to be kidnapped and killed has already

been mentioned. This is also evident in the fact that the risk of dying for a male aged 20-24 is 4.5 times that of a female. In fact 60 percent of male deaths are caused by homicides (Romero, 1997). The number of widows, therefore, appears to be growing exponentially. In the year 1994, 73,000 children were reported to be without fathers.

Another common impact of the endemic violence on families and communities is displacement. "Displacement" refers to the aggressive takeover of land and property, forcing the residents to flee for their lives. In Colombia, guerrillas, paramilitaries, and/or drug dealers commonly use violence and extortion to take control of land. There are no effective safeguards. It is not uncommon for whole communities to be forced violently and urgently from

Box 5.1   Comuna Trece: Mariana's story of life after displacement

"I lived in El Salado and the houses were falling down because of the rain and we lived on a very steep hill, in high risk as they say, but also there were a lot of problems of violence. So they relocated many families, and we came to Comuna Trece.

"This was very hard, because, since we had to leave in a hurry, we had to leave almost everything and we had almost nothing for the new place. We knew very few people in the barrio.

"Very soon after we moved the guerrillas and paramilitaries took over the community and killed many people. In one month they killed my brother, a nephew, and another one disappeared. This is very hard; one was 18, the other 20, and my brother 37.

"We had no work. We had to register at the office for displaced people to receive some money for food, but this was not enough. My three children were full of fears and did not sleep well. They never went out, even to school, because they were afraid to be killed.

"One day we had a visitor. When he was leaving, we went into the street to help him find a taxi. He was gunned down in front of us. We never knew why! It is hard. But we cannot keep focusing on what has happened to us. We would become crazy.

"When CINDE came with the program, we started doing things to change what was going on. We started getting together every week to solve those problems we could not solve alone. We learned about the institutions in the community that could provide some health, nutrition, and income generation services.

"Most importantly, we became aware of what we could do for ourselves at home and with the neighbours. We learned to do a lot of things with our children. Now I feel much better. I understand better where to go and who to ask for help. But I am still scared that shootings could start again."

Mariana (not her real name)

their homes and belongings. These communities and families never get the chance to return. They are suddenly impoverished, homeless, and disenfranchised — and need to find another place to start a new life. Many end up in urban ghettos called barrios.

Human rights watchers have estimated that close to three million people were displaced in Colombia in the decade ending 2002. Displacement is unpredictable, taking place under conditions of extreme distress, fear, and panic. Most families leave their land empty handed. Displacement destroys community and cultural attachments. Citizens end up in alien environments — cut off from family, work

opportunities, and/or sources of support (RSS, 2003a; El Tempo, 2003). Moreover, displaced families also tend to relocate to barrios which are already overcrowded and impoverished. The lack of systemic documentation about displacement and displaced persons make it virtually impossible for government services to address their needs in any integral way. Barrios are not safe for families and children.

In addition, in the past decade illegal "armed groups" have become as common in the cities as in rural areas. These groups often target areas inhabited by displaced people where government presence is lacking or ineffectual. Sometimes self-defense groups develop to fight off the invaders. Both groups have access to guns

Box 5.2   Comuna 13: Barrios war "Worse than a scene from Hollywood"

Comuna 13 is in a very strategic location in Medellin — on the route in and out of town. Food and munitions for surrounding regions need to travel through Comuna 13. In addition, this area is a corridor for an important highway that connects with the mega in the west. Those who control the route control a great geographical range. Both the guerrilleros and opposing paramilitary groups want control over this strategic area.

There was a time when the armed groups moved in. In response, community "self-defense groups" developed to protect the Comuna. Armed confrontations became a daily occurrence. At any time of the day and into the night, wherever you were, bullets would be flying by you. It was like a terrifying episode at the level of the most violent scenes in Hollywood movies. Madness walked the streets armed with submachine guns and pistols, with its face hooded so that only a glimpse could be caught of a look full of rage, hate, thirst. There, in

those barrios with ridiculously steep streets that give the impression of being stairs to heaven, hell itself had a branch office.

The self defense co-oped the young people and performed a "cleansing." Cleansings consist of actions in which delinquents, drug addicts, and prostitutes are forced to leave a zone. This is achieved through forced eviction and, in some cases, murder. Eventually they succeeded in driving the armed groups and the groups of common delinquents out of the barrios. But there remain people who sympathized with the armed groups. Some of the members of the groups created networks and settled here — supporters helped them with a lot of things.

Things have calmed down. Right now there are sporadic killings — by dagger, by blade. It isn't very common, but sometimes you are talking to people and they say, "Can you believe it? There have been 12 knife killings in my barrio."

Adapted from a report by:
Sandra (Family and Community Center Worker, CaC program, Comuna 13)

and other weapons. A kind of "barrios war" takes place. In some barrios this has gone on for years.

The stresses and lack of support in barrios can give rise to rage, calls for vengeance and, out of frustration, to domestic violence. Young children in these areas are witnessing or experiencing high levels of physical and sexual abuse. Poverty, malnutrition, morbidity, and lack of schooling are further outcomes associated with displaced families. Perhaps most tragic is the fact that cultural identity tends to be lost along with land and community. When groups are forcefully scattered, mobilization, leadership, and the ability to participate in community building are destroyed. This represents systemic and sustainable annihilation of the social fabric (Rodríguez y Bodnar, 2006).

The plight of children

Displacement is particularly alarming for women and children. In 2002, 49 percent of the displaced homes were headed by a woman. Women are being forced to assume responsibility for the affective and economic well-being of their families, while being cut off from supports and dealing with hostile, often violent environments. (RSS, 2003b). Their situation puts their children at risk.

Displaced children suffer from loss of family members, loss of friends and peers, and, in overcrowded and impoverished conditions, are often subject to physical abuse and exploitation. Most displaced children cannot access schooling (Research Group, 2000). In the capital city Bogotá, it has been estimated that up to 77 percent of displaced children are not attending schooling of any sort. Moreover, for some ethnic groups the problems are compounded with Afro-Colombians being a case in point. It has been estimated, for example, that less than 21 percent of this population are accessing supports for housing, food, and education.

Living as a displaced person during childhood can have long-term consequences. Children without schooling during their formative years have no structure to their day and no focus for their energy; no way to educate themselves and no help in applying rational thought or finding other ways to work through their emotional trauma. It is within this context that children are left to build their personal and cultural identity (Petit, 2003). Even if and when the children are in places of relative safety, their environment tends to be filled with symbols and reminders of violence. Meanwhile, for many, adults are unable to provide protection and security, and domestic violence is rife. Many displaced children end up in armed groups — as soldiers, assistants, and/or in situations of domestic and sexual slavery. It is estimated that between 7,000 and 13,000 children below the age of 18 years in Colombia are working with armed groups (Forero, 2003).

Children whose feelings of chaos and danger are not addressed, who have no way of developing a vision for a better future, and who are deprived of a sense of territory or homeland, have no foundation upon which to build a healthy world outlook. Instead, they generate fantasies, attitudes, and values which reflect their context. Brutality affects the trajectory of their lives and relationships with others. It is those with weapons who seem to have power. They are the source of admiration and envy. Knowing no other way of being, children as victims become perpetrators — and the cycle of violence continues. CINDE believes that interventions in the early years of life can avert this path.

Colombians helping Colombians: Family and Community Centers (FCCs)

For 30 years, CINDE has been running programs to facilitate healthy physical and psychological environments for children, their families, and communities within the most excluded areas of the country. We in Colombia who have lived through terrifying days and nights want to move on. But deep scars remain. For us, the only way to transcend the horror is to reconstruct the social fabric within communities. No outsider can make this happen. That is why we have called our program *Colombianos Apoyando Colombianos* (CaC) (Columbians helping Colombians). The CaC program is a grassroots approach to dealing with individual and community problems. At the core of the program are Family and Community Centers.

The role of Family and Community Centers is to foster environments for holistic development in young children. Describing the work of the Family and Community Centers is difficult because FCCs do not follow any set formula. Each Center is established on the basis of existing services in the community, gaps in service provision, or access and the aspirations of the community. FCCs are committed to capacity building; that is they reflect methods that complement what already exists in the community, incrementally adding value and addressing needs as they develop.

Each center is run by a Coordinator and supported by several Promoters. These are respected individuals from the community who take on the task of "leading" community development projects. Promoters meet weekly with the caregivers and children to identify and find ways for addressing family- and child-related issues within the

Box 5.3   Strengthening the abilities of families and communities to attend to the physical and psychological needs of their children

One of the goals for the Family and Community Centers is to strengthen positive and nurturing interactions between parents and children. The Promoters conduct weekly meetings for caregivers focusing on the needs of children from birth onward. They also conduct the *Play to Learn* and *Peace Builders* programs for young school-age children. These Programs use participatory methodologies to model, raise awareness about, and build values for peace and democracy.

Adult programs are focused on enhancing their understanding about how children perceive the world, and how to meet their psychosocial needs at each stage of development.

One of the best tools for parent-child relationship building is our *Parent Toy Library* whereby families are introduced to educational toys and games and take these home to share with children, siblings, and others in the community. Parents are also taught about the use of drama and art as ways to help children work through stress and trauma. Parents discuss activities which will enhance cultural identity and improve self-concept for all family members.

Other child-oriented issues which are prevalent in each community are discussed in groups, and families are given support to work on community-oriented solutions for common problems. While caregivers, including mothers, fathers, and others are meeting, the children have access to play areas with trained workers. Here children have opportunities to work through their own issues, to socialize in positive ways, and to develop logical thinking and pre-literacy, pre-numeracy skills through a structured learning environment.

Another function of FCCs involve the facilitation of support networks for fathers, mothers, and other significant people who have common goals of improving the environment where children live.

community. The Coordinators and Promoters receive training from CINDE, depending upon their situation and needs. Topics may include community organization and participation, networking, inter-institutional articulation, and/or leadership. Training on child development and programming for young children is also provided.

Activities of the FCCs

FCCs have identified diverse program needs for displaced families and other victims of violence and disruption. Some programs focus on psychosocial needs such as trauma and post-trauma sessions for children and families and/or the restoration of self-esteem at the individual and collective levels. Many communities in Colombia continue to experience intergenerational waves of violence. New, younger gangs are replacing the old ones. For this reason,

FCC programs address strategies for modifying violent imageries and deeply rooted negative behaviors in children and young adults through participatory approaches that address strengthening values for peace and democracy. Other programs have a more pragmatic focus such as the support for income generating projects. Some programs tend to be common for all FCCs, such as the Parent Child Toy Lending program in every FCC.

Once communities have prioritized their own health, cultural, educational, and political needs, they develop a plan of action which includes the mobilization of people and other resources. If extensive financing is needed, the members of the FCC will seek alternate funding sources as part of their plan. Private sector sources and philanthropic agents are enlisted to assist with early childhood and

Box 5.4   FCC promoters speak out

"We received a lot of training. We met every week to learn about the different aspects of running a centre: how to keep it organized, how to conduct meetings, about how children grow and develop, and how to treat common illnesses in children like diarrheic, respiratory diseases, and first aid."
Dora Yanet Osorio of Maruchenga

"What I like most is to see the mothers coming to the meetings every week, very happy because they are learning many things to raise their children: they do not scream at them, show affection, children behave better; also because they do not have as many problems with their neighbours. Now they can dialogue."
Beatriz Guzman of Maruchenga

"The children don't get diarrheic as often and those who are already in school are achieving better and don't miss school as often."
Nayerlin Velasquez of Comuna Trece

"I always admired the program. I was surprised to see how everything we learned at the meetings, we applied immediately working with the families. We learned to diagnose the needs of the families, to make health campaigns, to conduct home visits. We conducted the meetings in any place of the community, because we did not have the Center yet."
Claudia Gomez of Maruchenga

"I started as an assistant and I just supported the Promoter in some activities in the program. Then I helped with the attendance and the materials, including lending the toys to the parents, and later I became a Promoter in charge of conducting the meetings for 20 or 25 mothers and meeting with the institutions of the community. Now I can help my family and I am interested in continuing learning."
Luz Amparo Garcia of Comuna Trece

family programs. In this way FCCs move beyond social service facilitation to community development, fostering inter-sectoral solidarity to meet the needs of young children and their families. Private sector sources and philanthropic agents are mobilized to assist with early childhood and family programs.

Characteristics of the FCCs

Family and Community Centers have characteristics which contribute to effective outcomes. They differ from traditional child care centers in several ways:

- Their clientele is seen as the family (and community) rather than the individual child.
- Their target population includes families with children in early infancy.
- They take a holistic perspective — assessing impact of programs in terms of cultural and social relevancy as well as immediate alleviation of issues.

FCCs offer an alternative social pattern to that of violence and abuse, modeling democratic, consensus decision making which focuses on benefits of a broad population. Because they are not tied to a hierarchy or bureaucracy, members of FCCs can undertake quick decision making and action. Most importantly, the FCCs are totally localized: each one determines the specific needs of their community and involves locals who "own the problem" to develop strategies for addressing these.

Networking for community support

CINDE has worked to facilitate networks amongst FCCs. Through networking, individual FCCs can build on each other's experiences, and, where possible, share resources. CINDE also plays a facilitation role for communication, sharing, and cooperation *between* FCC and other relevant agents and agencies. Networks which facilitate dialogue between civic agencies, non-government organisations, and government departments are usually highly successful in terms of planning, securing funding, coordination, and taking action.

Colombia appears to be increasingly stable and may be ready now to undertake a review and development of national and regional policies that address social inclusion, prioritise services for children within family structures, restore rights, and support a focus on prevention over crisis interventions for delinquency, abuse, and intra-family violence. Family and Community Centers are delivering programs and creating networks whereby diverse social sectors connect with each other, coordinate activities, strengthen institutional arrangements, and develop financial strategies. This mobilization of agents and services under the auspice of better environments for children represents a decentralized power base from which the establishment of local and national policies for children and families can emerge.

Sustainable infrastructure: Developing leaders in early childhood education to influence national policies

The Family and Community Centers reflect a strategy for conflict-ridden communities to rebuild themselves through a focus on their children. They represent a grassroots approach to helping themselves, despite a lack of government and other resources and support. As the Promoters become more confident and more successful in implementing local programs, they seek out other Promoters and extend networks. CINDE is facilitating this process. The goal is to develop a nationwide community safety net and support system through the FCC scheme.

But CINDE is aware that sustained progress calls for leaders at all levels of society — we need those who can rebuild communities, and also those who can influence regional and national policies towards the development of a new social fabric. From the beginning, CINDE has been working through universities in Colombia to develop a cohort of leaders who understand the critical nature of support and healing in the early years of life.

Box 5.5   Changing communities one step at a time: From drug addiction to helpful participant — Carmen's story

"When Carmen initiated her participation in the FCC program she was a drug addict. At the beginning she was very quiet, never participated or interacted with anyone. However, she never missed a meeting and paid attention to everything.

"In one of the meetings we were talking about self-concept. She started to cry, and I was very concerned about what was happening to her. When the meeting was over I asked her why she had cried so much. She said that the meeting had made her aware of all the problems she had, the ugly life she was living, and how bad she was feeling.

"She told me some things about her life. Her family did not like her, and she had been thrown out several months ago, and she did not have good relationships with her four brothers and sisters. Her boyfriend wanted to marry her, but he was the one that introduced her to drugs. Now she was stealing and selling the objects to buy drugs.

"After that I started a new relationship with her. She began to be interested in cooperating with me in the meetings, keeping attendance control, and going with me to do the home visits. One day, when I was walking to the office, a man I did not know greeted me in a very friendly way and thanked me for having Carmen in the program. According to him, she had changed so much, that she was now living again at home and was having good relationships with everyone in the family. That man was Carmen's father.

"Carmen, started changing rapidly, and she went from being a volunteer, to becoming a Promoter, and eventually becoming the Coordinator of the program, elected by her own colleagues. Now her family and children live peacefully and productively."

Story told by Claudia Acevedo

The development of specialists and leaders in the fields of early childhood and social development is being forwarded through CINDE and its partner universities in a unique program. Following our philosophy of relevance, openness, and flexibility, we use a theoretical practical approach that combines conventional educational delivery with innovative and participatory learning strategies aimed at producing social change and transformation. To earn postgraduate qualifications, students will undertake community and social development projects, be involved in research and evaluation projects, and participate in processes for formulating and implementing policies and programs.

We need a different outlook for the next generation. Our community development programs, our focus on young children, and our unique educational opportunities for early childhood leaders are, we believe, creating a way towards a better future for the children of Colombia (Arango, et al., 1992).

Lessons learned

There are many things that can be learned from the development and working of Family and Community Centers. Four key lessons are worth drawing out and highlighting here.

Local initiatives are most effective

The Family and Community Centers in Colombia are not highly resourced, nor are they dependent on outside funding and charity. Rather, what makes them effective is the fact that they are locally developed and run. They are staffed by local individuals who are committed to ensuring healthy environments for children and who have good communication, interpersonal, problem solving, and leadership skills. Training is provided to raise awareness about processes for developing programs and strategies. Training also includes information dissemination about topics which are important for all Centers, such as child development and dealing with traumatised children and caregivers. Networking within communities and between FCCs is fundamental in creating a new social fabric for a troubled region.

Simple programs can have multiple outcomes

Parent-child toy libraries provide educational opportunities for young children. However, they also serve as a facilitating vehicle to discuss child development issues with parents. Through the toys, parents are encouraged to talk and play with their children. Older siblings are often included. The parent-child toy libraries also provide a network for caregivers; facilitating discussions and information sharing amongst mothers and between mothers and promoters/specialists.

Those affected by conflict have the greatest power to overcome and heal

The Colombians helping Colombia program has shown that despite their own troubles, citizens can be mobilized to address community needs. Colombians care about the health and well being of the future generation. The cycle of violence is being broken through activities which empower and support

---

Box 5.6   Focus on the future

Three Family and Community Centers are functioning in Comuna 13. Their names were chosen by the community. This is significant. The barrios are doing all they can to erase its violent past and focus on building a new "story" for the community. The CFCs call themselves *Sowers of Hope* in Gabriela barrio, *The Children's Future* in Corazon barrio, and *Dream Fulfillers* located in Independence barrio.

---

mothers and teachers who work with the children. By ensuring equitable access to good services, by modeling peace in community centers, by introducing play and joy for children and those around them, the process of healing and peace can take hold.

Strategies used for reconciliation and peace need to target the whole community and to provide an integrated approach to meet diverse needs

In Colombia, whenever possible, the displaced families have called upon relatives and friends for physical, financial, and emotional support. Whole families may move in with their supporters — causing depletion of sparse resources. Further, the non-displaced relatives and supporters tend to absorb the stress and anxiety of those within their care network. Frustration and resentment can ensue. FCCs however have the potential to offer community-wide programs which can address the needs of all families, both those directly and indirectly affected by conflict.

Chapter Six

Nepal: Kishor Shrestha's Story

Nepal is a small landlocked Himalayan country sandwiched between China to the north and India to the east, west, and south. For just over 100 years, and up to the early 1950s, it was ruled by the autocratic Ranas and remained totally isolated from the outside world. Since 1951 and the first popular revolution to overthrow the Rana regime, Nepal has experienced significant political turmoil. For the past decade this turmoil has resulted in a prolonged period of violence as Maoist rebels have waged a "People's War" against the government.

During this time, a concerted campaign by a network of NGOs has achieved much success in advocating for children. One tangible result has been the establishment and recognition by all factions of "Children as a Zone of Peace" and a commitment to avoid activities that may harm children. During this period a Resource Center for Early Childhood Development has also been established at the Research Center for Educational Innovation and Development (CERID) at Tribhuvan University with the support of UNICEF Nepal. Over the last few years the Center has begun contributing to this advocacy work through conducting research on the effects of the conflict on young children and also disseminating the findings of that research to help inform the development of effective policies and programs for young children and their families.

In this chapter Kishor Shrestha tells the story of how the political turmoil and violence have been impacting young children and their families and about the success associated with the establishment of "Children as a Zone of Peace." Kishor is a researcher and Associate Professor at CERID and has been the coordinator of the Resource Center established there since its inception. In discussing his most recent work, Kishor reflects upon the important role that research can play in advocating for young children and families in conflict-affected societies, as well as the significance of developing international networks, in this case through the World Forum on Early Care and Education.

Nepal: La historia de Kishor Shrestha

Nepal es un pequeño país en los Himalaya situado entre China con la cual linda por el norte, e India país con el linda por el oriente, occidente y el sur. Por más de 100 años, hasta los primeros años de la década de los 50, fue gobernada por los autocráticos Ranas y estuvo completamente aislado del mundo exterior. Desde 1951 con la primera revolución popular que derroco el régimen de los Rana, Nepal ha experimentado una significativa turbulencia política. Durante la década pasada esta turbulencia resulto en un prolongado periodo de violencia debido a que los rebeldes maoístas entablaron una "Guerra del Pueblo" contra el gobierno.

Durante este tiempo, una campaña concertada por una red de ONGs ha obtenido mucho éxito en hacer abogacía por los niños. Un resultado tangible ha sido el establecimiento y reconocimiento por parte de todas las facciones de la "La Niñez como Zona de Paz" y el compromiso por evitar acciones que puedan hacer daño a los niños. Durante este periodo se estableció un Centro de recursos de Desarrollo Infantil Temprano situado en Centro de Investigaciones para el Desarrollo y la Innovación Educativa (CERID) en la Universidad de Tribhuvan con el apoyo de UNICEF Nepal. Durante los últimos años el Centro ha empezado a contribuir a esta tarea de abogacía a través de la investigación sobre los efectos del conflicto sobre los niños/as pequeños y de la diseminación de los resultados de la investigación para ayudar al desarrollo de políticas y programas efectivos para los niños/as pequeños y sus familias.

En este capitulo Kishor Shresta cuenta la historia de como la turbulencia política ha estado impactando a los niños/as pequeños y a sus familias y acerca de los éxitos obtenidos con la implementación de la "La Niñez como Zona de Paz". Kishor es un investigador y profesor asociado en le CERID y ha sido el coordinador del Centro de Recursos. Al discutir su trabajo mas reciente, Kishor reflexiona sobre la importancia del papel de la investigación en la abogacía por las poblaciones de niños pequeños y sus familias en sociedades afectadas por el conflicto, así como o sobre el significado del desarrollo de redes internacionales, en este caso a través del Foro Mundial en Educación y Cuidado Infantil Tempranos.

Setting the scene: Political conflict in Nepal

Nepal is a small Himalayan country with a total population of about 25 million people and covers an area of around 147,000 square kilometers. Between 1846 and 1951, the country was ruled by the autocratic Rana regime and remained totally isolated from the outside world (Rizal & Yokota, 2006). In 1951, the Rana regime was overthrown by a popular revolution supported by the King, and an agreement was reached whereby King Tribhuvan would play the role of a constitutional monarch under a new democratic constitution to be framed by a constituent assembly elected by the people (Karki & Seddon, 2003). Unfortunately, the election for the constituent assembly never happened and the next 40 years were marked by political revolts and turmoil between the monarchy and various political parties.

The roots of the present conflict can be traced back to 1990 and the establishment of a new constitution following a political uprising. This new constitution created a constitutional monarchy and made the government responsible to the people. At one level the constitution was regarded as very progressive, guaranteeing fundamental rights for the people of Nepal and opening up opportunities to entertain civil rights. It certainly gave rise to high expectations among the people and led the country from being closed and authoritarian towards being more open and democratic.

However, the governments of the post-1990 period tended to be unstable and failed to introduce the socio-economic changes that were increasingly becoming expected by the people (Karki, 2003; Rizal & Yokota, 2006); nor could they take visible measures against corruption, social-ethnic discrimination against "dalits" (untouchables), and minority ethnic groups. Such lack of progress simply fueled the concerns that some had with the 1990 constitution itself. The Maoists in particular had rejected the original constitution, feeling that it was an inadequate basis for what they called genuine democracy; and they continued to demand a constituent assembly. The lack of consequent progress was simply regarded as proof of these concerns.

In 1995 the Maoists presented a 40-point list of demands to the Prime Minister. The demands were broadly similar to the demands made by all of the opposition parties (Karki & Seddon, 2003). Some of the demands in the list included calls for:

- Nepal to be declared a secular state
- girls and women to be granted rights to parental property
- all caste-based exploitation to be terminated
- *dalits* to no longer be treated as untouchables
- a right to free expression and freedom of press and publication.

Shortly after presenting this list of demands, the Maoists began their "People's War" against the government that lasted for the next 11 years. Originally, the Maoists had strongholds in the far and mid-western regions of Nepal; but these have spread to the extent that they now have control of almost all of the rural areas of the country and have an armed force known as the People's Liberation Army, totaling an estimated 35,000.

Initially the Maoists pledged equality, freedom, and justice for Nepal, and they focused their campaign on attacking corrupt officials and village headsmen. They also fought against the age old discriminatory behaviours towards women, the poor, and the "dalits" and attacked social anomalies like gambling, consumption of alcohol, wife bartering, and corruptions that were rampant in the society. Because of this, they gained significant support, especially from the "dalits" and "janjatis" (indigenous people who tend to be socially and economically marginalised), as well as women (Raj, 2004). Indeed, it has been estimated that about a third of the Maoist fighters and militias are women (Upreti, 2004).

However, while agreeing with many of their political demands, people increasingly became fearful of the

Maoists as they developed and expanded their tactics. They began to attack police posts and army barracks and took away arms and ammunitions. They raided government offices in the district headquarters and they looted banks. They also attacked local government offices and destroyed their buildings. Innocent people were increasingly finding themselves caught in the crossfire. Moreover, there were instances of both Maoist rebels and government forces using local people as human shields; and it was quite common to find schools being taken over by both sides for use as meeting places and shelters.

Politically the Maoists instituted their own government, known as the people's government, and appointed people mostly from "dalits" and "janjatis" as the heads of this government. They compelled local landlords, rich people, office bearers (including school teachers) to pay taxes in the name of donations. They also made it mandatory for the local people to participate in the mass meetings they organized in their stronghold areas. They abducted school children and teachers for short periods of time with the aim of indoctrinating them into their ideology.

Things came to a head in 2004 when the King dissolved parliament and took over the executive power himself and formed a new cabinet with himself as the head. This created a discord between the democratic political parties and had the effect of bringing the Maoists and political parties to one platform. The bottom-line demand of the Maoists for a constituent assembly became the demand of all the political parties, too, and was reflected in a 12-point pact signed between the seven main political parties and the Maoists. A mass movement was launched to restore the democratic system. Peaceful protests sparked off in the capital and some urban areas spread across the country within a short time. During this time, a number of civilians lost their lives owing to indiscriminate firing and baton charges by government forces. About 5,000 people were also injured, some of them badly.

Despite a curfew imposed by the King, millions of people took part in the protests. Eventually, the King stepped down and reinstated the dissolved parliament and returned the executive power to the people. The government stopped calling the Maoists "terrorists," disclaimed the "bounty" on the heads of the Maoist leaders, and asked Interpol to remove their names from the list of terrorists.

The new government is in the process of forming an interim government that will also include the Maoists. At the time of writing, the process of holding the election for the constituent assembly is in the offing. The government and Maoists have agreed to keep their arms under UN surveillance until the election is held and a new full democratic constitution is drafted. In order to resolve the process of peaceful negotiation, the rebels and the government have declared a ceasefire. The people of the country are hoping for peace and political settlement. The UN has shown its willingness to monitor the ceasefire and keep vigil over the arms and activities of the rebels and the government for a free and fair election for the constituent assembly.

The effects of conflict on children and families

At the time of writing Nepal is, therefore, slowly emerging out of conflict and is beginning to work at rebuilding an open and fully democratic society. However, the 11 years of violence associated with the "People's War" have left a huge legacy. For such a small country, Nepal has experienced a relatively high loss of life, including many children. Moreover, thousands of children are having to deal with the trauma caused by witnessing the brutal killing of family members and neighbours and with having to endure other violent events.

Beyond these immediate effects of the conflict, the 11 years of war have impacted the children's lives in four additional ways. The first has been the break-up and often complete disintegration of families. It is

estimated, for example, that 8,000 children have been orphaned because of the conflict. Many more have seen their families torn apart as they have had to flee their homes and villages for fear of their lives.

Male family members, in particular, have been forced to leave their villages to evade being caught up in the violence and the risk of being forcibly recruited by the Maoists or taken away for interrogation by government forces. In some of the village homes there are only old people, women, and children (Raj, 2004). This, in turn, has led to many families struggling to survive as they no longer have the human resources required to earn a living through agricultural work. All of this is compounded in some instances by the fact that much of the local infrastructure — such as Village Development Committee offices, roads, bridges, vehicles, telephone repeater towers, banks, and government offices — has been destroyed through the conflict.

Following on from this, the second key impact of the conflict has been to create thousands of families that are now internally displaced. Many of these initially fled their own homes and villages; but now, with the

Box 6.1 Effects of the "People's War" on children and families

During the 11 years of insurgency:

- 14,000 people have been killed

- 460 children have lost their lives and a further 535 have been injured

- 8,000 children have been orphaned

- 40,000 children have been displaced

Source: CWIN (2006)

ceasefires, find it difficult to return home. Many are unwilling to return home having seen their houses burned to the ground and their cattle being killed or taken away. Others have witnessed their family members and neighbours tortured or killed. Most of the displaced children have said that they do not want to return home (CERID, 2006). For their parents another barrier to returning home is that the life in the rural village is very hard. There is no basic infrastructure; no electricity, no road, and no drinking water, and, of course insufficient food. Therefore, despite the call from the Maoist rebels to return to their homes, most of these people are not willing to do so.

The third key impact the conflict has had on children is the ongoing sense of fear that they feel and the restrictions this places on how they can go about their daily lives. Reports continue of children becoming injured and killed because of explosive devices left behind after the encounters. However, many more are

Box 6.2   The use of early marriages to protect daughters

In some of the villages some parents follow the practice of early marriage of their children. Early marriage is marriage below the age of 18 years for girls. But there has come a change in this practice over the years owing to an increase in the awareness level of rural people and government law against child marriage. Recently, as the result of the conflict, some of the parents found themselves forced to get their daughters married at an early age although they knew it was against the law. Asked why they did so, they said that the rebels usually did not force married girls to join them. In another story, which was published in a newspaper some time back, some of the school-going girls dressed up like married women in order to be camouflaged and avoid being forced to join the rebels.

having to learn to trust again and to begin regaining their confidence. For many, their only experience has been one where they have not been able to play freely and explore outside for fear of being abducted or caught in the crossfire. During the conflict, for example, it has been estimated that 31,000 children and teachers have been taken away by rebel groups for certain periods of time in order to indoctrinate them. Similarly, 254 children have been arrested by the state security forces for interrogation (CWIN, 2006). Other children have seen their parents go to elaborate lengths to protect their older brothers and sisters in order to prevent them from being forced to join the rebel Maoist forces.

The fourth and final key impact of the conflict on children's lives is in relation to its effects in restricting children's access to education. It has already been mentioned, for example, that schools have often been taken over by both rebel Maoists and government forces for meetings and shelter. For some children, schools are no longer seen as safe places; and it will take some time for them to regain their confidence and feel comfortable going back to school.

Drawings sketched by an eight-year-old child reveal some of the alarm he has been experiencing in the school. His drawing of the school before the conflict showed how it was seen as a fun and happy place. He and his peers could play outdoors with play materials in a free and fearless atmosphere. However, his drawing of the school after the conflict showed how it was being shadowed by clouds of gunfire smoke with no play material available. There are people with guns around the school and the community. Interestingly, in the second picture he shows that even the sun is being covered by clouds.

During the period January 2005 to May 2006 and before the ceasefire, it has been reported that bunkers were built in at least 56 schools, a further 31 schools were affected by bomb explosions and at least eight schools were destroyed by setting fire (CWIN, 2006). Some schools are still directly experiencing the presence of the security forces in their vicinities and

Image 6.1   An 8-year-old child's drawings of the school before and after the effects of the conflict

Box 6.3   Children in schools learn with guns around them

Even though the government expressed its commitment to recognize "Children as a Zone of Peace" (CZOP) some three years ago, school children in eight schools across the country are still compelled to continue learning in buildings manned by armed security personnel and with security posts set up inside them. Moreover, at least in three other schools barbed fences are still in place even though security personnel have left the school buildings.

Source: The Kathmandu Post, June 27, 2006

are suffering security obstructions — even after the security personnel have left the schools.

All of this continues to limit the ability of schools to operate properly. For example, school supervisors and resource persons who are responsible for supervising and providing technical support to the schoolteachers are not visiting schools regularly due to security reasons. Schoolwork days have considerably lowered because of repeated strikes and "bandhs" called by the rebels and other political parties. A school is required to open for at least 230 days a year, but over the last couple of years the schools are hardly operating for about 150 days a year. This has directly affected the efficiency of the school management and the quality of education.

Moreover, many children who have been displaced from their native villages due to the conflict are completely deprived of the opportunity of attending school. Those who are fortunate enough to go to school are having to deal with problems related to language and social adjustment. One study conducted recently has shown that children who have been internally displaced are often neglected and humiliated at school and in the classroom. These children prefer the back seats of the classroom and do not interact much with the teachers and other children. The study has reported cases of children dropping out of school caused by the unfriendly behavior of their classmates (CERID, 2006).

"Children as a Zone of Peace" campaign

One of the distinguishing features of the conflict in Nepal has been the tendency for both Maoist rebels and government forces to take over and use schools. This, in turn, has led to significant concerns being raised by journalists and human rights organizations who have led a concerted campaign aimed at highlighting the effects of conflict on children and educational institutions. A report published by the Institute of Human Rights Commission Nepal, for example, found that in 11 top daily newspapers taken together as many as 573 news items on children in armed conflict were published between January 2001 and December 2003 (IHRICON, 2003).

Moreover, this news coverage trend has been consistently growing since 2001. Some of the popular daily newspapers have given as much as 25 percent of their total space for the news on children in armed conflict. Many journalists have put their lives at risk while collecting news, and some of them have been killed. The issue of children in conflict has therefore found its way onto the national agenda. The continuous reports of atrocities and human rights violations published in the newspapers have not only educated the general people about the conflict and its effect, but publication of such news has also forced the conflicting parties to pay attention to the extensive violation of child rights and human rights.

In 2002 these concerns were crystallized into a campaign known as "Children as a Zone of Peace" that represented a coordinated effort on the part of a number of organizations in Nepal. The major thrust of this campaign was to lift the children out of the conflict and not to use them in any activity related to it. The campaign soon developed into a national movement guided by major international human rights tenets and has involved advocating to and monitoring all the parties involved in the armed conflict in Nepal (SC/Norway, 2006).

Under this campaign the government, the political parties, and the civil society are all urged to respect and abide by ten main resolutions aimed at safeguarding the physical and emotional well-being of children. Pamphlets and booklets were produced and circulated widely and many meetings and discussion sessions were organized as part of the campaign. All of these activities helped to ensure that the key resolutions associated with the campaign gained much publicity across the country.

Box 6.4   Ten resolutions of the "Children as a Zone of Peace" campaign

1. Declare educational institutions as zones of peace and do not use school premises as venues for any sort of political activities.

2. Declare a ceasefire on children-specific occasions such as children's day, education day, international child rights day, and during the health camp, etc.

3. Do not obstruct the fundamental services meant for children such as education, health and vaccine, food, etc.

4. Protect vehicles carrying children. Do not attack school and public buses used for commuting children.

5. Do not create problems to the programs and activities in which children are participating.

6. Do not produce and put materials such as news, pictures, and rolling images in the mass media that affect children's psychology.

7. Respect the rights of children and do not discriminate between them on the basis of the political affiliation of the parents.

8. Give preferences to children's need for relief, rehabilitation, and assistance.

9. Do not obstruct the flow of humanitarian aid agency services to the children.

10. Include peace education in the school curriculum and develop a culture of peace.

The "Children as a Zone of Peace" Campaign has been the result of a coordinated campaign among many organizations including: UNICEF Nepal; Save the Children Alliance; CWIN; and Seto Gurans National Child Development Services.

Officially, all of the warring factions associated with the conflict accepted the resolutions associated with the campaign. There is certainly a widespread feeling that this has led to a reduction in the tendency for children to be drawn into and affected by the conflict. In particular, the campaign has, to a large extent, helped to keep the conflicting parties away from the educational institutions including early childhood set-ups and has dissuaded the conflicting parties to use children in the conflict.

Role of research in advocacy campaigns

One of the consequences of the success of this campaign has been the development of strong networks of organizations advocating for the safety and well-being of children. Directly as a consequence of this campaign, a National Coalition for Children as a Zone of Peace was formed with the aim of addressing wider issues associated with children caught in armed conflict. To date it has been able to raise awareness and provide shelter, education, and counseling services to some conflict-affected children. Similarly, a committee known as Children in Conflict Coordination Committee, comprising around 20 organisations, was formed to coordinate the activities of various organisations working in the area of children and conflict.

It is within this context of a growing and strong advocacy network for children's rights and well-being that work at the Resource Center for Early Childhood Development has developed in new ways over recent years. The Resource Center was initially established at the Research Center for Educational Innovation and Development (CERID) of Tribhuvan University in 1997 with the support of UNICEF Nepal. From the beginning, my role was to act as coordinator for the Center and to oversee its development. Initially, the activities of the Resource Center were limited to organizing training programs (for the teachers and parents); undertaking research studies; convening dialogue sessions, workshops, and seminars; and publishing bulletins.

Even though the conflict in Nepal over the last 11 years has been particularly intense and violent, it was a relatively new phenomenon in our context. Its impact on children, families, and education had, therefore, not been a concern for educationists, teachers, and parents in Nepal until the recent years. This was also true for the Resource Center. Initially our primary concerns were:

- how to develop outreach early childhood services to the children living in remote rural areas
- how to influence the government plans and policies
- how to ensure the quality of early childhood services.

However, my involvement in the World Forum on Early Care and Education has played a key role in helping me develop expertise at the Resource Center

and begin focusing on the needs and experiences of children and families affected by conflict. One of the main benefits that participation in the World Forum has brought has been the opportunity to develop strong links with other academics and experts in the field of early childhood studies. In 2004, with the help of the World Forum Networking Fund, we were able to develop links with Dr. Wayne Eastman and enable him to visit the Center. Moreover, with the support of the World Forum, Dr. Eastman and I have established a new academic journal, the *Journal of Early Childhood Development*, that is helping to promote early childhood research and disseminate findings across Nepal.

Since 2002, and again through the World Forum, I have been able to work with Professor Diane Levin on the effects of media violence on young children. From this work I have written papers on media violence and presented them at the last two World Forums. We have also jointly organised discussion groups on media violence and children during the World Forums. While preparing papers and moderating discussion groups, Diane generously provided support to me by reviewing my papers and suggesting group work. She also provided a lot of reading materials — some written by herself and some by others. Those materials have been good resources for me as well as for others who visit the Resource Center.

Moreover, all of this work has increased my research interests in the conflict in Nepal and its effects on children and families. It was also through Diane that I came to learn about and was invited to participate in Working Forum Belfast. Working Forum Belfast met in 2004 in Belfast, Northern Ireland, and brought together early years professionals and researchers from a wide range of countries affected by conflict. The Working Forum was facilitated by the World Forum Foundation in partnership with NIPPA – The Early Years Organisation based in Northern Ireland. The theme, "Building Bridges: Healing Communities through Early Childhood Education" enabled us to share experiences about the many different ways that conflict impacts children and their families and to learn about strategies used for work with children and families in other countries experiencing conflict.

Working Forum Belfast led to the establishment of the International Working Group on Peace Building with Young Children. The Working Group has met on several occasions since, and this current book is one of the initiatives of the Working Group. The other activities that the Working Group has been involved in, and its future plans, are described in more detail in the last chapter of this book.

My own participation in Working Forum Belfast in 2004 and subsequently as a member of the International Working Group on Peace Building with Young Children proved to be invaluable in giving me deeper insights into how conflicts in other countries affect the lives of young children. Moreover, exposure to various programs being implemented and tried out to support children and families in dealing with the impact of conflict has broadened my knowledge of violence affecting children's lives. As a result, I have developed two important new initiatives at the Resource Center:

- collecting information and documents on how children and families are being affected by conflict in Nepal and documentation of the programs being run by various organizations across the country
- conducting research on the impact of conflict on children and families.

Working together with my two other colleagues, we are now building up a significant resource of materials at the Center. Moreover, through this work the Resource Center is now also in a position to begin supporting others engaged in research on the effects of conflict on children and families by providing research grants to the students of higher education doing research work and to non-governmental organisation staff. Recently, we conducted a study on the situation of the children displaced by the armed conflict, some of the findings of which have been discussed above. This study has helped to reveal some of the devastating effects that the conflict has had on families and how many have disintegrated.

More generally, the Resource Center has established a national network of over 20 organisations across Nepal that are involved in the implementation of early childhood programs. The network was originally set up 10 years ago and has been concerned with sharing and disseminating good practice. In the last few years, and as a result of my involvement in the Working Forum Belfast, the network has become increasingly concerned with the impact of the conflict on children and families. As part of this, the Resource Center also actively advocates the philosophy of the "Children as a Zone of Peace" by organizing discussion sessions, disseminating information, and displaying booklets and reports in the Center itself.

At the time of writing, a key element of my work in the Resource Center is to support individuals and organisations that deal with the conflict-affected children and their families. The information and documents we have collected are being made available through the Center, and people can visit the Center and use the resources available here to develop programs for helping the affected children and families.

As a part of the research grants program, we will continue to provide technical support to the students of higher education and non-government organisation staffs to enable them to undertake research work in the field of early childhood development and conflict, and will be disseminating new knowledge to the officials responsible for formulating policies and to other stakeholders who draw up and implement early childhood development programs especially focused on children and families affected by the conflict.

Lessons learned

As I have described in this chapter, the recent history of Nepal has been one characterized by political instability and turmoil. For the last 11 years this has erupted into armed conflict, resulting in the deaths of many thousands and the break-up and, in many cases the disintegration, of families and whole communities. Children have been caught up in all of this, not only as direct casualties of the violence itself but also as witnesses to it. The trauma experienced by many children because of this has been exacerbated by the tactics of both rebel and government forces who have used innocent people as human shields and have taken over schools as places to meet and to organise themselves.

As with all conflict-affected regions, much hurt has been caused, and deep physical and emotional scars have been left behind. While Nepal is moving into a post-conflict era and there is growing hope for the future, these scars will take years to heal, as will the damage done to whole communities and families. While it is an intensely sad and depressing picture, there are also key lessons to be drawn out from our situation that are important for other early years organisations caught up in conflict-affected societies. Perhaps the main lesson from Nepal is the importance of professionals, the government, and the NGOs being willing to accept and respond to the need of children affected by the violence.

In particular, the example of the "Children as a Zone of Peace" campaign provides an excellent illustration of the power and influence that organisations can bring to bear when they work together and advocate on behalf of children and families. The ability of organisations to develop effective networks has been essential in providing people with the necessary support and confidence to be able to promote the needs and rights of children. In addition, and with this emphasis on advocacy, my own experience over the last few years has taught me the importance of research in helping to identify and document the needs and experiences of children and families, with a view to informing and influencing government policy and the development of new programs.

Finally, the role that the World Forum has played in relation to my own work also highlights the importance of making links internationally. Particularly through my involvement in the Working Forum Belfast, I have been able to develop my knowledge and expertise in relation to the effects of conflict on children and families and am now in a position to begin passing this on through research and also the many other activities being organised through the Resource Center. The ability to draw upon the international experience and expertise of other members of the International Working Group on Peace Building with Young Children has been, and continues to be, invaluable in helping us at the Resource Center focus on the needs of children and families and advocate effectively on their behalf.

Chapter Seven

Northern Ireland: Siobhan Fitzpatrick's and Eleanor Mearns's Story

Northern Ireland is a small country emerging out of a prolonged period of armed conflict. For the last decade, and since the first paramilitary ceasefires were called in 1994, efforts have been made to reach a political settlement between the two main traditions in Northern Ireland — Catholics and Protestants. The 25 years of armed conflict that preceded these ceasefires, however, has left a legacy of a society that is now deeply divided. While the guns may have fallen silent, Protestants and Catholics still tend to live in segregated communities, send their children to segregated schools, and celebrate different events.

NIPPA – The Early Years Organisation, was founded in 1965 just a few years before Northern Ireland erupted into violence. During the 25 years of violence it has worked consistently to meet the needs of children and their families on both sides

of the political divide. Indeed, it has been one of the very few organisations in the region to provide a shared space for people from both traditions to meet and share their experiences and support one another. Today, NIPPA has over 1,000 member groups located in communities across Northern Ireland and is playing a key role in fostering reconciliation and helping to build the peace in the region.

In this chapter, Siobhan Fitzpatrick and Eleanor Mearns tell the story of NIPPA's origins, how it developed through the years of conflict, and what role it is now playing in promoting respect for diversity among children, families, and communities through the innovative programme, the *Media Initiative for Children — Northern Ireland* (Peace Initiatives Institute). Siobhan is currently the Chief Executive of NIPPA and has been in this post since

Irlanda Del Norte
La historia de Siobhan Fitzpatrick y Eleanor Mearns

Irlanda del Norte es un pequeño país que esta emergiendo después de un prolongado periodo de conflicto armado. Durante la última década, y a partir de los primeros llamados al cese al fuego de los paramilitares en 1994, se han hecho grandes esfuerzos

por llegar a un acuerdo político entre las dos principales tradiciones en Irlanda del Norte: los católicos y los protestantes. Los 25 años de conflicto armado que precedieron este cese al fuego han dejado como legado una sociedad profundamente dividida. Aun cuando los fusiles permanezcan silenciosos, los protestantes y los católicos todavía tienden a vivir en comunidades segregadas, envían a sus hijos a colegios segregados y celebran fiestas diferentes.

NIPPA – la Organización para los Primeros Años, fue fundada en 1965, algunos años antes de que surgiera la violencia en Irlanda del Norte. Durante los 25 años de violencia ha trabajado consistentemente para satisfacer las necesidades de los niños, niñas y sus familias a los dos lados de la disputa política. De hecho, ha sido una de las pocas organizaciones que proveen un espacio compartido donde la gente de las dos tradiciones se puede reunir, compartir sus experiencias y apoyarse recíprocamente. Hoy NIPPA tiene más de mil grupos asociados, localizados en comunidades a lo largo de Irlanda del Norte y esta jugando un rol clave en el apoyo a la reconciliación y a la construcción de paz en la región.

En este capitulo Siobhan Fitzpatrick y Eleanor Mearn, cuentan la historia de los orígenes de NIPPA, como se desarrollo a través de los años del conflicto y que rol esta jugando en la promoción del respeto por la diversidad entre los niños y niñas, sus familias y las comunidades a través de un programa innovador, La

Iniciativa para los *Niños a través de los Medios — Irlanda del Norte* (derechos de autor: Instituto de Iniciativas para la Paz). Siobhan es actualmente la Directora Ejecutiva de NIPPA y ha sido su directora desde 1989. Eleanor ha trabajado con NIPPA desde 1990 y durante los últimos 3 años ha compartido la responsabilidad por la coordinación de la Iniciativa de los Medios para los Niños y las Niñas, Programa para el Respeto por la Diferencia. Antes de esto, Eleanor trabajo como especialista en niñez temprana, dando apoyo consejo y capacitación a una variedad de grupos. Ha estado involucrada en el trabajo de NIPPA de consulta a los niños para obtener sus puntos de vista en temas relacionados con las políticas de infancia, tanto en Irlanda del Norte como en la Republica de Irlanda. Eleanor también hace parte de la división internacional de la organización y ha trabajado con niños, niñas y comunidades en Europa Oriental. Antes de unirse al equipo de NIPPA Eleanor manejaba un Centro de atención a la niñez temprana en Belfast.

1989. Before this Siobhan spent five years working as an early years advisor supporting the development of community models of early years services in Northern Ireland. Prior to joining NIPPA, Siobhan worked in health and social services management. Eleanor has worked with NIPPA since 1990 and, for the last three years, has been jointly responsible for the co-ordination of the Media Initiative for Children, Respecting Difference programme. Before this, Eleanor worked as an early years specialist providing support, advice, and training to a range of early years groups. She has been involved in NIPPA's work on consulting with children to seek children's views on early years policies in Northern Ireland and the Republic of Ireland. Eleanor is also part of the organization's international division and has worked with children and communities in Eastern Europe. Prior to joining NIPPA, Eleanor managed an early years centre near Belfast.

Background to Northern Ireland

Northern Ireland is politically part of the United Kingdom and geographically located in the north-east corner of the island of Ireland. It is a small country, covering just over 14,139 km^2 and with a population of just under 1.7 million people. It is a deeply divided country with the vast majority of the population belonging to one of two groups:

- "unionists" who are the majority (53 percent) and who tend to be Protestant and regard themselves as British
- "nationalists" who constitute a sizeable minority (44 percent) and who tend to be Catholic and regard themselves as Irish.

For 25 years, from 1969 to 1994, Northern Ireland experienced a prolonged period of armed conflict involving paramilitary groups representing both traditions and also the British Army. Republican paramilitary organisations waged an armed campaign during this period with the aim of driving Britain out of Northern Ireland and thus creating a "united Ireland" with the Republic of Ireland. On the other side was the British Army protecting the interests of Britain in the region, as well as a number of loyalist paramilitary groups whose aim was to defeat republican paramilitaries and to protect Northern Ireland's position as part of the United Kingdom.

During this period, over 3,600 people were killed and well over 40,000 more were injured as a result of the violence (Morrissey & Smyth, 2002). Much of the violence during this time was indiscriminate and included city and town centre bombs detonating with little or no warning and a significant number of what were known at the time as "doorstep killings" due to the fact that victims were often shot dead at point-blank range when simply answering their front door (Fay, et al., 1999).

Not surprisingly, and given the nature of the violence, high levels of residential segregation emerged as people either moved to areas they felt more safe and secure in or were actually burned out of their homes and forced to move by those living nearby from the other ethno-religious community. It has been estimated, for example, that just within the first few years of the violence (1969-1972) between 8,000 and 15,000 families were forced to leave their homes and live elsewhere (Smyth, 1998: 15). Moreover, and as Boal (1999) has identified in his broader analysis of urban trends in the region, there was a "ratchet effect" whereby intense periods of violence tended to significantly increase levels of segregation that would then never return to their previous levels during later times of relative peace (see also Murtagh, 2002; 2003). It is also important to note that much of this violence and the highest levels of segregation that have emerged because of this have tended to be concentrated in areas within Northern Ireland that were already suffering from

social and economic deprivation (Fay, et al., 1999; Morrissey & Smyth, 2002; Smyth & Hamilton, 2003).

Since the first paramilitary ceasefires were announced in 1994, Northern Ireland has experienced just over a decade of relative peace, and all sides to the conflict are making efforts to secure a political settlement. However, the legacy of 25 years of violence has remained. Social and residential segregation remain a characteristic feature of Northern Ireland society, with the 2001 Census revealing that a quarter of all local wards (25 percent) consist of populations that are at least 90 percent Catholic or Protestant and well over half of all wards in Northern Ireland (58 percent) having a population that is at least 75 percent Catholic or Protestant. Moreover, the vast majority of schools (some 95 percent) remain segregated, and it is still quite common to find young people reporting that it has only been since they have gone to university that they have had the opportunity to mix socially with those from "the other side."

Given such levels of segregation it is not surprising to find that there remains significant levels of ignorance, fear, and mistrust harbored by those on both sides towards one another. This, in turn, can often fuel sectarian prejudice. Moreover, tensions between some neighbouring Protestant and Catholic communities remain and tend to be punctuated by incidents of stone throwing and sporadic violence. Even at the time of writing (May 2006), the local news carries a report of a 15-year-old Catholic who was savagely beaten to death by a gang of Protestant young men wielding baseball bats for no other reason than he was Catholic and in the wrong place at the wrong time.

NIPPA – The Early Years Organisation

NIPPA – The Early Years Organisation, was founded in 1965, just a few years before Northern Ireland erupted into violence. In those first few years it reflected what was happening in England at the time in that it was led mainly by middle class, private providers whose main aim was to set up private pre-schools to meet a need in their communities. However, things began to change in 1969 when the violence began; and it soon became much more of a community-based movement that provided an opportunity for parents to unite around the interests of their children, as opposed to sectarian and other political divisions. Most significantly, early years services became a place where children and families could be safe with each other and begin to explore their differences in supportive environments.

Thus, while NIPPA's role initially was to help the private sector, the emerging conflict had the effect of re-focusing its work and approach towards one that was underpinned by a strong community development ethos. The emphasis for NIPPA, therefore, soon shifted towards helping communities to organize and develop their own pre-school groups. Perhaps one of the most significant aspects of NIPPA's work during these years was its ability, as an organisation run largely by women, to work "under the radar screen" to begin creating an alternative space to the violence and division caused by the conflict. At that time the early years sector was not being funded and, therefore, was not being fought over by the power brokers in terms of the Catholic church or the controlled education sector. Rather, it was being run by women who were motivated by the simple but powerful need to create a new experience and an alternative space from the conflict for themselves and their children.

Within this alternative space the opportunity was therefore created for women from across the divide to meet to share experiences and perspectives and to support one another. This was made possible by the fact that NIPPA was organized into 19 branches across Northern Ireland with between 20 and 30 local pre-school providers being members of each. Many of these providers were located in segregated areas; and, therefore, branch meetings provided the space for Catholic and Protestant playgroup leaders and parents to come together and to share experiences

and support one another. We could clearly see the importance of this shared space, for example, in the aftermath of the IRA's bomb in Enniskillen when a lot of our colleagues in the local area of Fermanagh knew those who were killed. They had some connection with community playgroups, and the local branch was used as a vehicle for people to talk about the awful atrocity of that. Once people got to know each other in that sort of environment, then the cementing and building of relationships really began to happen. This is one of the reasons why it has been possible for NIPPA, in more recent years, to begin taking a leading role in promoting reconciliation and respect for diversity.

NIPPA and the peace process

By the time the first paramilitary ceasefires were announced in 1994, NIPPA had developed into an organisation that was well placed to make a significant contribution to the "peace process" that followed. Not only were we already facilitating cross-community work between early childhood practitioners, but our actual size — around 1,000 member groups located across Northern Ireland in communities of all backgrounds — now meant that we had significant potential to begin to effect a community change model.

This potential was quickly recognized soon after the ceasefires were announced, when we, as an organization, were asked to be an intermediary funding body for the European Union's Special Support Programme. This Programme consisted of a significant amount of funding provided by the EU to invest in the social and economic fabric of Northern Ireland and thus to help consolidate and build the peace. NIPPA's role as an intermediary funding body was, and still is, to support the early years sector in Northern Ireland by overseeing a total investment of £40 million ($76 million) over the next ten years.

With this significant new role and also with the renewed impetus created by the peace process, we were able to reconsider more fundamentally our approach to reconciliation work and what role we as an organisation could play within this. For many years, NIPPA had adopted a clear "non-sectarian" and "non-political" approach in relation to its work and the shared spaces it created within this. However, the peace process had now created the opportunity for us to move beyond this and promote a more explicitly "anti-sectarian" approach that involved overtly naming and challenging sectarianism and encouraging respect for diversity. We recognized, however, that this was going to be extremely difficult given the physical and emotional scars that people carried with them from the past 25 years of conflict. While our groups were already doing a lot of work around respecting differences, this tended to be in relation to issues such as race and disability; and there was definitely a reluctance and in many cases a fear of dealing with our own "ism."

Fortuitously, at the time we were working on developing a more explicit approach to dealing with the divisions between Catholics and Protestants, an influential research report was published in Northern Ireland looking at the attitudes and awareness of 3-6 year old children in Northern Ireland (Connolly, et al., 2002). The report, entitled *Too Young to Notice?*, showed that even at the age of three, children were beginning to be affected by the divisions that exist and to internalise the cultural preferences and attitudes of their respective communities. Moreover, and by the age of six, these attitudes were found to have become much more entrenched and negative.

Also at this time, and independently of all of this, David McKay and Paul Harris of the Peace Initiatives Institute (Pii) were visiting Northern Ireland. Pii was established in Colorado (USA), to explore ways of contributing to building peaceful societies in conflicted areas of the world through a focus on children and young people. Pii's vision was to "create a different dialogue, different understanding, and less strife among populations in conflict throughout the world." Many of the founding members of Pii had a business background and believed that their media

skills could be used to good effect to promote such a message, but that this had to be combined with work through the school curriculum. An important early decision for them was that effective work would require the development of partnerships with local organisations and leaders who had insight into the conflict and culture of local situations.

Thus, just as we were looking at ways of doing something different and being more explicit, we were contacted out of the blue by Pii. They talked initially about wanting to work with older children. Our initial feeling was that it is nearly too late then, and that we have to start with younger children, and that

---

Box 7.1   Young children's attitudes towards those from across the divide

"They (Catholics) rob."
Protestant girl, aged 4

"It's a bad person (Protestants) because they want to kill all the Catholics."
Catholic girl, aged 6

"Catholics are the same as masked men; they smash windows."
Protestant girl, aged 4

"Catholics don't like Protestants and that's why they don't like them — they're bad."
Catholic boy, aged 6

"That one's just yucky (referring to British Union flag). I hate English and I love Irish."
Catholic boy, aged 6

"It's the Fenian flag (Irish Tricolour). It's only bad people that have that colour of flag."
Protestant girl, aged 6

Source: Connolly, et al. (2002)

this could also be easier. This was also the feeling of many of the other participants at the first meeting in Northern Ireland facilitated by Pii; and very soon, therefore, the decision was made to focus efforts on the early years.

Not long after this Pii approached us and said that what we were doing, what we wanted to do, and the way we were thinking fit in with exactly what they wished to achieve. We, therefore, began to explore with them how we could work together. Alongside bringing people together and acting as a catalyst for change, Pii definitely brought with them their expertise in the media and their desire to use the media. We would not have done that ourselves. We would have just thought it was too expensive and that we would never be able to get funding to do that. However, we also brought with us our extensive knowledge and experience of working with young children and families. Initially Pii's main concern was to produce cartoons for broadcasting that promoted respect for differences among young children. They had not really thought about complementing this with outreach work. However, when they heard what we were already planning to do in relation to developing curricular materials for use with children and parents, it was agreed that these two things could fit together well.

The *Media Initiative for Children — Northern Ireland*

Through this partnership between ourselves at NIPPA and Pii the *Media Initiative for Children — Northern Ireland* was born. One of the key people at NIPPA who was involved in the initial meetings facilitated by Pii and who had a significant influence on the original framing and development of the *Media Initiative* was Carol MacNamara. Tragically, Carol died suddenly and unexpectedly after only a few months of work. However, her vision and absolute commitment and enthusiasm for the programme have definitely remained.

Over the next few months three 1-minute cartoons were designed and produced by the *Media Initiative* based around four characters playing in a park. The cartoons themselves can be downloaded and viewed online at: www.mifc-pii.org. Each cartoon dealt with a particular aspect of difference — the first addressed issues of physical differences (disability); the second focused on racial differences; and the third on cultural differences (sectarianism). Each cartoon began with a playground scenario where someone was being excluded and/or where children were playing separately and then modeled inclusive and pro-social behaviour. The main message in all the cartoons was the same; that you respect difference whatever that difference is and it is okay to be different; diversity is good and should be respected and embraced. We chose these three differences to get started, but they could have been any differences.

There was some disagreement at that time as to whether it was a good thing to broaden the approach like this. Some felt that the media messages should concentrate specifically on cultural differences

Jenny, Jim, Kim, and Tom: The four main characters from the Media Initiative for Children — Northern Ireland.

between Catholics and Protestants. However, it was eventually agreed that focusing just on differences between Catholics and Protestants would have been very hard to sell to practitioners. Also, many NIPPA groups were already trying to do something on diversity; and so it was much better to build upon what they were already doing rather than just introducing something completely new that they had not tackled before.

The actual development of a resource pack and accompanying curriculum for use with the outreach work was the responsibility of one of us (Eleanor) together with another colleague at NIPPA — Sinead McShane. We felt that it would be very good to give playgroups resources and lot of activities or suggested activities to do with the children. The idea was to give them a turn-key package, because we knew from previous experience of doing this type of work that it can be very hard and time-consuming to find suitable resources reflecting diversity to use with the children. The idea of the turn-key package was, therefore, to give the groups a lot of the initial resources so they could start the work immediately and then allow them to build upon these themselves.

The pack that has been developed includes a range of resources and suggested activities including: hand puppets representing the four cartoon characters with changeable faces to allow the children to explore different feelings; jigsaw puzzles depicting a wide variety of cultural events and symbols, including those associated with the Protestant and Catholic communities; sequencing cards to help children understand and discuss the storylines from the three cartoons; lotto cards; posters; and feelings cubes that have the faces of the cartoon characters on each of the sides of the cubes and allow further exploration of feelings.

Box 7.2   Comments from parents about the *Media Initiative for Children*

"The programme introduced children to differences in a gentle manner and has made my child more aware of the thoughts and feelings of others."

"A very positive initiative to educate young children."

"We thought it was a good idea especially since we adopted our daughter from Bulgaria and have experience of race and cultural difference."

Alongside encouraging the children to explore differences and respect diversity, perhaps the other key theme underpinning the resource pack is a focus on feelings. Although children have the feelings, they cannot always articulate them. They do not even always know the body language associated with the feelings, so we felt that a big part of the core of the work should be around the feelings associated with being left out and excluded.

Children in a NIPPA playgroup playing with materials from the resource pack.

Key lessons learned from delivering the *Media Initiative*

The cartoons were first broadcast on television in Northern Ireland and the Republic of Ireland early in 2004, and the resource pack was piloted during this time in 10 early years settings. There are four key lessons that we have learned to date through this pilot that are worth drawing out briefly here.

The importance of training playgroup leaders in how to use the resource pack

The first lesson was the need to provide training to help playgroup leaders know how to use the resources and exercises. We learned that people need a lot of ideas about how to use the resources to get the most out of them, and they do need to be careful because you can use the resources in a wrong way. For example, some people were concentrating far too much on the differences within the characters and highlighting them; and that has led us to talk now about first of all thinking about the similarities before looking at the differences with the children. In relation to the character with a disability, for example, we are now suggesting that he can be first introduced to the children as a boy who comes to playgroup and loves playing with the Lego®, who loves to go swimming on Tuesday night, and one day a week he loves to go to the park with his grandmother. So you try to get all of the similarities in first of all and then you can say he has to wear a corrective eyepatch, but that is okay as he has a sore eye. What we found was some groups, because we weren't giving them enough guidance in the beginning, were saying to the children, "Now why do you think they won't play with Tom?" and because the children weren't saying too much at all they said, "Is it because he's got an eyepatch?"

Within this, one specific issue that has arisen regarding the resources has been the fears that some playgroup leaders have had around using the resources relating to differences between Protestants and Catholics. In some cases they were unsure about what they were actually supposed to be doing. We had to do a lot of work to reassure them, because some of them thought they were nearly expected to teach politics in some way to young children. We stressed that all the resources do is to provide children with the opportunity to increase their knowledge and awareness of the range of sports and social activities that the different communities in Northern Ireland engage in.

The importance of encouraging playgroup leaders to reflect upon their own attitudes and experiences

A second key lesson from the pilot was the recognition that in order to effectively deliver the *Media Initiative*, playgroup leaders need to begin reflecting upon their own attitudes and beliefs. On the one hand, some work was required in order to convince some of the playgroup leaders that this work was necessary in the first place. For example, one of the arguments that came up in the beginning was that the children are too young for this type of work. To address this, we now do an exercise in the training whereby the playgroup leaders are asked to think of their first memories of difference. We start by getting them to think about their very first day at school, and then we ask them to remember the first time they ever noticed someone who was different from themselves. Each time we have done this, we find that the stories and the dialogue that comes out from this shows that they themselves have memories of difference from maybe four and five; and maybe their experiences with the adults around them has not always been a good experience.

On the other hand, it has also been found to be necessary to increase the playgroup leaders' own understanding of the events and symbols associated with the other community and, moreover, being comfortable with discussing these. If people are going to do work around diversity with young children then they need to look at themselves first of all and their own values, attitudes, prejudices. We have certainly been picking up that the biggest fear among playgroup leaders has been the cartoon focusing on cultural differences between Protestants and Catholics, so we have done a lot of work around that. Perhaps the most significant part of this has been the provision of an additional day of training where we have brought in a trained mediator and community relations expert where the playgroup leaders from both sides of the divide are asked to sit and talk to one another about cultural difference. People are asked to bring in symbols and things that represent their own cultures, and there is a lot of dialogue and discussion around this. What we have found is that this provides an excellent way to discuss how they can then use the materials in the resource pack relating to cultural differences between Catholics and Protestants.

The need to provide playgroup leaders with ongoing support

A third key lesson learned to date is the need to provide ongoing support to those playgroup leaders delivering the *Media Initiative*. At NIPPA this has led us to provide training to our own Advisers so that they can then provide effective support to their playgroups. We feel this works in two ways. First, the more the Advisers know about the *Media Initiative* and the more they get involved, the more they can support and help the groups and the parents out there. Second, and following on from this, we are hoping to get funding to provide additional resources to Advisers so that they can support the work that the playgroups are doing directly with the parents.

In relation to this last point, there is certainly still a lot of anxiety and a lack of confidence among some playgroup leaders surrounding work with parents. They are worried about what they should do if a parent comes in and says that she or he does not want the child doing some of the activities associated with the other community. During the training, you can definitely see that there is worry there; you can see it from the body language. However, I feel we have certainly become a lot better now in terms of providing training and support, and that this could be helped further if we had the opportunity for the

Advisers to be more directly involved in supporting the playgroup leaders' work with the parents.

The importance of research and evaluation

We have already touched upon the importance of research in relation to the influence that the publication of the *Too Young to Notice?* report had in helping to confirm the need for us to do more explicit diversity work in this area and in providing evidence that we could use to help guide the development of the *Media Initiative* (see Connolly, et al., 2002). However, research has continued to play an important role in relation to the evaluation of the pilot programme and the further development and refinement of the *Media Initiative*. While we do not have the space to discuss it in detail here, we did ensure that the pilot programme was rigorously evaluated, using an experimental design so that we could develop a clear sense of what the actual effects of the programme have been on young children's attitudes and awareness. What the evaluative research showed was that the programme did have a positive effect in relation to a number of key outcomes we had identified for the project including:

- increasing children's ability to recognise instances of exclusion;
- increasing their ability to understand how being excluded makes someone feel;
- being more willing to play with others, including those different from themselves.

Further details on the evaluation have been published elsewhere (see Connolly, et al., 2006). Perhaps the key point to stress from this is the need for all of our work to be evidence-based and informed by rigorous research so that we have objective means of assessing whether the programme is actually working or not. Moreover, undertaking such research forces us to be clear about what the key outcomes are and what we wish to improve in relation to the programme.

Conclusions

In conclusion, the main message from this particular chapter is an extremely positive and encouraging one. It demonstrates the power of the early years sector and how effective it can be in working with children, families, and communities to help build peace. At the time of writing, NIPPA has trained over 200 preschool groups and an estimated 3,500 children have already had experience of some of the resources and activities associated with the *Media Initiative*. Indeed, regionally, market research indicates that about 70 percent of all children and parents in Northern Ireland have now seen at least one of the cartoons on television. Moreover, NIPPA remains characteristically ambitious and has set itself the target of making the *Media Initiative* resources available to all preschool settings throughout the island of Ireland by the end of 2007. As NIPPA is very much aware, however, for this to work there is the need to have a full infrastructure in place of training and ongoing support to these settings as well as ongoing research to inform the development and refinement of the programme.

As for the Peace Initiatives Institute, it is important to remember the critical role they have played as change-agents within the context of Northern Ireland and bringing the vision of developing a programme around the use of the media. They serve as an excellent example of how outside agencies can work effectively in helping to promote reconciliation and build peace in conflict-affected societies. The key to their success was not just having a clear vision but also being acutely aware of and sensitive to the needs of local people and organizations and being committed to the principle of working in partnership with them.

Perhaps the point to finish this chapter on is that it is clear from the experience of developing and delivering the *Media Initiative* that it is not the children who have the problem, but the adults. Preschool children are already actively involved in exploring and making sense of the world around them. They are more than competent and able to deal with the messages underpinning the *Media Initiative*, of valuing diversity, and respecting difference. As has been seen, it is the adults who struggle with this, often having to deal with the fears and psychological scars they are carrying from living through a period of violent conflict. However, what is so encouraging is that playgroup leaders and parents are keen to break from the past and they do want the best for their children. What this chapter has shown is that they are willing to take the steps forward necessary to achieve this, however uncomfortable these may be.

Chapter Eight

Palestine:
Ali Shaar's Story

Palestinians number about 10 million scattered all over the world in the status of citizens, refugees, and political asylums. Approximately 3.2 million Palestinians live in the West Bank and Gaza, the geographical area acknowledged by the international treaties to be the home of the Palestinian state. The peace process with neighboring Israel started formally in 1992 based on above mentioned treaties, but has gone through drastic, repeated failures that led to the eruption of a non-stop extreme wave of violence. *Al-Aqsa Intifada,* which started in September 2000 after the failure to agree on the final solution of the conflict, formed a tragic page in the history of Palestinians in terms of the severity of consequences on the lives of Palestinian families. The continuing conflict has homebred the efforts to establish the Palestinian state and its institutions, severely affected the health and well-being of Palestinians, and resulted in extreme psychological distress to several population groups with children being the hardest hit part of the population.

The chapter on Palestine will elaborate on the impact of the conflict on the lives of Palestinians in general, but will discuss in detail the impact on children in particular. It will discuss the dynamics and the extent to which Palestinian children were victimized in this ongoing conflict and will illustrate different programmatic interventions developed to combat the negative impact of conflict on the

Palestina:
La historia de Ali Shaar

El conflicto en Palestina es fundamentalmente político, afectando a tres y medio millones de personas que viven bajo la ocupación de Israel. La ultima oleada de violencia se ha desarrollado desde Septiembre del año 2000, después de un incidente asociado con la visita del Primer Ministro Israelí, Ariel Sharon, a la Mezquita de Al-Aqsa Mola. La Intifada actual ha continuado por seis años y al momento de escribir esto no parece tener una salida inmediata.

La violencia asociada a la Intifada se ha sentido a lo largo y ancho de Palestina. En Masaken, por ejemplo, una pequeña comunidad de aproximadamente 4,000 residentes localizados en la periferia de la ciudad de Nablus, han vivido los efectos directos del conflicto sobre la niñez. A partir de la exposición directa con el conflicto, niños y niñas han manifestado una variedad de respuestas que van desde el trauma y otras reacciones psicológicas adversas, hasta una tendencia a repetir eventos violentos en sus juegos. En respuesta a ello, la comunidad de Masaken se ha involucrado en crear un programa infantil para responder a las diversas necesidades creadas por la exposición a la violencia durante la Intifada en los niños, las niñas y sus familias.

psychological well-being of children. While many interventions were able to bring moments of relief to children, improve their ability to resilience and coping, it remained critical to stress that peace is the only pre-condition for balanced development of children.

Ali Shaar, a public health specialist, has worked for many years in Palestine both as a community practitioner and as a manager of health programs addressing the needs of marginalized groups in the West Bank and Gaza. During the *Al-Aqsa Intifada*, and as the health specialist at Save the Children Federation, he was involved in the design and execution of interventions seeking to alleviate the effects of violence, closures, and poverty on the children and their mothers in hard hit areas. In his chapter, Ali is reflecting on his experience in this field and is drawing the experience of dedicated colleagues, who were involved in providing care to those most in need.

Setting the scene:
The Al-Aqsa Intifada

The conflict in Palestine is fundamentally a political one where about 3.5 million people in the West Bank and Gaza are living under the occupation of Israel. The Oslo Agreement in 1993 provided the platform for the establishment of the Palestinian Authority that started to assume responsibility for services and governance in the West Bank and Gaza. Signing the agreement between the PLO and Israel was supposed to be the first step in solving the Palestinian and Israeli conflict through gradually opening the door for dialogue, trust building, and cooperation. For about seven years after the Oslo Agreement, the peace process went through many challenges and difficulties, leading to an ever-increasing level of frustration and loss of trust between the two parties about their real intentions and commitment to building peace in the area.

It was a special incident that occurred about six years ago, however, that triggered a wave of violence that was unprecedented and that is still going on. The incident centered around the visit of the then Israeli Government Minister Ariel Sharon to Al-Aqsa Mosque in September 2000. His visit had the full support of the then Prime Minister of Israel Ehud Barak and came just days after the failure of the Camp David talks between Israel and Palestine that were hosted by U.S. President Clinton. When Sharon visited the Al-Aqsa Mosque, the 3,000 soldiers who guarded him opened fire on demonstrating Palestinian prayers, killing eight of them. This, in turn, led to major political unrest in the country and the extreme use of military force by Israel that resulted in the deaths of many more Palestinians during the following few days.

Ariel Sharon's visit and the Israeli military response to the demonstrations that followed triggered the spread of what we now call the Aqsa uprising or the *Al-Aqsa Intifada* as it is called in Arabic. This Intifada has now continued for six years, and at the time of writing there seems to be no immediate end to it. This visit provoked such waves of violence because it was perceived by many Palestinians as the violation of one of the most holy places for Muslims after Makka. It also brought to a head the ever-increasing anger and frustrations experienced by many Palestinians who regarded it as symbolising Israel's refusal to comply with the Oslo Agreement.

The harmful impact of the conflict on children and families

There are five key effects that the Intifada has had on children and their families that need to be emphasised here. The first and most obvious effect relates to the children's dramatically increased exposure to violence. It is estimated, for example, that 700 Palestinian children have been killed since the events at Al-Aqsa mosque in 2000. For those children who have survived, many have either been injured or seen family members injured and others have experienced the painful loss of close relatives. When taking into consideration that the Palestinian population in the West Bank and Gaza is 3.2 million, then the 4,500 deaths occurring since September 2000 would be around 2 per thousand. Imagine what this figure means when translated with a bigger population: for instance, this would equal 500,000 deaths in a country the size of the United States. In addition, most of the children who were not directly exposed to the violence that occurred were indirectly exposed to it through regularly watching the news reports of the violence.

Alongside exposure to violence, the second main effect that the Intifada has had on Palestinian children and their families has been the marked deterioration in their health and living conditions. Since the Intifada, the health system has been faced with an unprecedented demand upon its already limited resources and has been faced with a range of

A woman giving birth at Qalandia Checkpoint 17th of February 2005.

problems that the system was not ready to cope with. This can be seen, for example, simply in terms of the huge number of casualties and the nature of their injuries. These demanded resources far beyond those available in the health system. Moreover, there were the closures of the borders with the West Bank and the isolation of 300 completely separated locations, with curfews that left people isolated in their homes for long periods of time. These closures, curfews, and movement restrictions imposed on Palestinians prevented health care professionals and patients from accessing services when needed. More than 130 people died because they were denied access to hospitals. And home deliveries increased to 30 percent of all deliveries compared with 5 percent prior to Intifada. Deliveries at checkpoints were documented on many occasions and the death of newborns and/or mothers resulted from many of these incidents.

Third, there have been the many psychological effects experienced by children as a consequence of the Intifada. Based on data from health institutions and observations in medical practice, there was an increase in psychosocial disorders in children under age 14 that were associated with exposure to violence. It was very hard for parents to see the psychological effects on the children and especially so given their feelings of helplessness and the inability to provide protection to their children. A significant increase in bedwetting started to appear. Aggressive

Box 8.1   Stories from Palestinian children

"Soldiers came into our house three months ago. They aimed their guns at my father's head and forced us outside the house. My father is sick and cannot walk. The soldiers did not believe him until they saw his walker. . . . I was very afraid about him, especially when two soldiers surrounded him with guns aimed at his head."

"Because I had no ID yet, the soldiers tied my feet to a Jeep and pulled me five times around a football playground. I had sore feet and knees."

"I saw the husband of my cousin killed. I could not sleep for a week and saw his bleeding whenever I closed my eyes. He was driving from a camp to visit his father-in-law's house. They shot him and the car he was driving fell down the mountain."

behavior in the children of all ages increased. There are also many children who demonstrated fear and psychosomatic disorders, such as sleeplessness, clinginess, aggression and angry outbursts, which started to appear at home, in school, and everywhere. Some have developed Post-Traumatic Stress Disorder — a common set of psychologically damaging stress behaviors that often appear in victims of or witnesses to violence, especially children.

Fourth, and following on from the psychological effects of the Intifada, we also quickly saw the impact of the conflict on the nature of the children's play. Both the boys and girls started to do a great deal of war-related play. It almost always followed the same theme of "Intifada games" with the children dividing themselves into two sides; the Palestinians were the "good guys" and the Israelis the "bad guys." During these games, children deployed terminology directly from the conflict including: "air attack"; "demolition crew coming"; "F16 plane"; "Apache helicopter"; as well as the use of Hebrew words. They also named and imitated some of the key characters associated with the conflict including: the former Palestinian leader Yasser Arafat (until 2004); the former Israeli Prime Minister Ariel Sharon (until 2006); and fighters, martyrs, and other personalities they saw on television.

The example of Ibrahim, a four-year-old boy, illustrates just how insidious the effects of the conflict can be on children's play and behaviour. His teacher described how he would sit cross-legged in the middle of the small playhouse shouting at his two classmates in a harsh voice. Every few seconds, his stern, aggressive words were punctuated by the thuds of toy plates or dolls which he had thrown on the floor. These three little children were playing one of the many "games" which reflect the violence Palestinian children experience in their daily lives in a war-zone. This particular "game" was an imitation of the procedure of invading and "searching" Palestinian homes, commonly practiced by the Israeli military in the Occupied Territories. Most of these children have the pattern memorized: the soldier bursts into the home and begins to shout at family members while randomly tossing furniture and other possessions across rooms.

After the Oslo Agreement, children in the kindergartens started to get back to an educational curriculum and atmosphere. The programs worked to support their development with a number of pioneering experiences promoting peace education. Children's drawings reflected clear progress towards hope, reconciliation, and balanced emotional life and we felt this reflected their improved experiences. It

---

Box 8.2   Research on impact of violence on Palestinian children

- 48 percent of Palestinian children directly have been subjected to some form of Intifada-related violence.
- 52 percent of children reported that parents couldn't protect them.
- 85 percent of the children thought that the future is bleak.
- In focus groups with parents the study found that:
  - 73 percent of the parents noticed psychological symptoms such as repeated nightmares, sleeping disorders, bedwetting, fear, anxiety, obsessive behaviors, hyperactivity, uncontrolled anger, and loss of trust in adults.
  - 48 percent of parents reported a change in quantity and type of play.
  - 46 percent reported anti-social behaviors.
  - 37 percent reported a drop in academic performance.
- In 34 out of 35 focus group discussions, parents reported feeling that they could not provide protection to their children.

Source: Save the Children (2003)

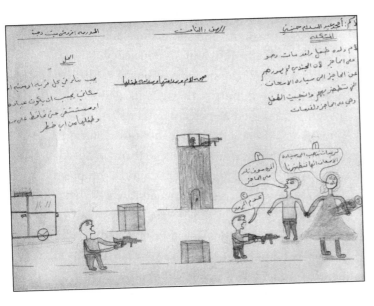

A child's drawing depicting the way to clinic as experienced by them during the period of closures.

was a very hopeful period. But then, after the Agreement failed, we started to see the results of the failure in the children's drawings, too. Their drawings began to show, once again, how they were trapped in the anxiety and fear that had developd. At the time of writing, their drawings are almost exclusively related to the prevailing situation with weapons, planes, and tanks appearing frequently, because this is what has become the normal life for the majority of our children.

Fifth, and finally, the Intifada has also affected children by contributing to rising levels of poverty, with all the resulting risk factors that poverty can bring. The political deterioration immediately resulted in a worsening of the economic conditions of the families living on the West Bank. With the closing of border crossings, curfews, and movement restrictions, people were not able to reach their

---

Box 8.3 The effects of Post-Traumatic Stress Disorder on children

When young children experience a traumatic event involving death, serious threat, or serious injury, they respond to the trauma. Their common immediate reactions are: a fear of being separated from the parent, crying, whimpering, screaming, trembling, and excessive clinging, trouble falling asleep. Children may also begin using behaviors from earlier ages, such as thumbsucking, bedwetting, and being afraid of darkness. The reactions are likely to be especially intense when the trauma is directly connected to trusted adults or the child's immediate situation.

Some children develop Post-Traumatic Stress Disorder (PTSD) from the traumatic event. PTSD is diagnosed when the following symptoms are present for more than a month:

- Repeated signs of re-experiencing the event through play or in trauma-specific nightmares or flashbacks.

- Routine avoidance of reminders of the event (such as photos of the harmed person, refusal to go to the location where the trauma occurred) or a general lack of responsiveness to normal situations.

- Hyper vigilance involving increased irritability, intense fear, poor concentration, regression to younger behaviors, becoming easily startled or angry, and sleep disturbances.

Experts generally recommend that children showing symptoms of PTSD receive professional help from counselors. However, this is not available in many communities where children are affected by violence, thereby increasing the potential harm caused by the trauma to children's long-term development.

For further information see EMSC (no date).

homes or their work places, and hence unemployment started to increase rapidly. This has affected the household income, especially for people dependent on the labor market in Israel for their income. By the year 2002, the social economic indicators revealed that around 50 percent of the population lived under the poverty line of $2 per person per day, and the unemployment rate reached 67 percent. The unemployment rate reached the extreme rate of 80 percent in some communities, especially those in Gaza. Because of lack of work opportunities, exhaustion of family financial reserves, and a reduction in the capacity of extended-family ties to provide social support, about 60 percent of the population started to be dependent on food aid as their means of securing this very basic need.

The spread of unemployment and severe increase in poverty rates had a dramatic effect on the well-being of the population. It especially affected children and women because of its impact on the structure and function of the family as the primary social unit. The man, who is typically the bread earner, has stopped being so because of the lack of work opportunities and restrictions on movement to work outside their own communities. In addition, the male population is a clear target for arrest, killing, and/or wounding, resulting in short-term or even long-term disabilities that clearly affect their ability to support their family and children. The ability of the father to play the protection role is severely damaged because, as perceived by both the children and adults, fathers can no longer provide protection to their children or families, as they are themselves victims. Hence, many men end up vulnerable to becoming victims of powers beyond their capacity to face. Last, but not least, the absence of appropriate skills to manage their own stress and the stress within their families contributes to their inability to help their children when they come under stress.

The multiplier effect of violence, closures, and consequent poverty was demonstrated in the health status indicators of the population in general, and also in relation to those associated with children in

particular. We saw a three-fold increase in the occurrence of malnutrition and anemia among children and women. Vitamin A deficiency, a disease that under normal circumstances should not be present in a community such as the Palestinian community, reached 22 percent in school-age children. Children with chronic diseases requiring regular medical care and expensive treatment, such as those with cancer and diabetes, almost completely lost the chance for accessing needed care and, hence, deteriorated or even lost their lives as a result of long-time neglect. A small study conducted to explore the health status of 20 children with diabetes revealed that one of them died as a result of acute complication of the disease, four others were hospitalized for severely compromised control of sugar, and none were able to maintain proper control of their blood sugar levels, which left them vulnerable to life-threatening complications.

Increased poverty and unemployment prevented people from utilizing alternative medical services as they could not afford them. It led to people delaying the start of needed care. This, in addition to strict barricading of communities, made it hard for anyone to leave for services outside communities, and resulted in the death of about 130 people at checkpoints or on the way to hospitals. The majority of those deaths were infants, mothers, and chronically ill people.

An early childhood program responds to children's and families' needs

I live in the community of Masaken. It is a small community with about 4,000 residents. This community is located in the peripheral part of the city of Nablus and forms the eastern entrance to the city. For more than six years, the Masaken community has been, and still is, suffering from violent experiences. It has a refugee camp close to it and has been subjected to many incursions and clashes with Israeli soldiers. For the vast majority of the year 2002-2003, it was under complete curfew — people were not allowed to go outside their houses. During this time, a number of people from the neighborhood were killed for going outside their homes.

I remember one time leaving my home in an ambulance that picked me up to take me to work in Jerusalem. I ended up spending two weeks at the office in Jerusalem because my return back home was usually difficult and many times not allowed. When I did get back, my wife and family told me that they were still under curfew without any relief. Tanks were always present, watching the area. The result of this situation was to create severe anxiety for many local people and especially for the children. There was no possibility of their being able to leave their homes or to play safely. This is when we started to think about the concept of developing what we began to call "Safe play areas for children."

I began working in Masaken to try to create an early childhood program that addressed the diverse needs of the children and families that have been created by their exposure to violence during the Intifada. We wanted to develop a program that responded to the needs of early childhood care, to the special needs that were arising from being in isolated areas, and to the desire to improve the psychological well-being of children. We therefore tried to provide the children with a "safe zone," a place where they could play and, to the best extent possible, be safe. We planned to design and build a safe play area where children could access toys and games, and where they could participate in group activities structured to relieve anxiety and stress. Through funding provided by the Gates Foundation and other agencies, a children's center was established and furnished to host early childhood activities and mainly to offer children a safe area to play and relief from their anxiety and stress.

The project was later supported by funds that enabled us to also develop community activities such

as extracurricular activities, games, drawing festivals, and sports. We also developed training courses and workshops for mothers to help them become involved as volunteers in the children's education process. The mothers also helped design the interventions that the project was aiming to achieve.

One example that stands out was a training workshop designed for mothers that taught them how to make puppets at home using simple, easily

Safe play area established in Al-Masaken neighborhood after the military incursion to the area in 2002.

available materials. They also learned how to use the puppets with their children in order, among other things, to help them work through and come to terms with their experiences. Another thing we did was help the mothers organize "open play days" where their children could get together to play and be busy as a way to ventilate stress and try to forget about the violence around them.

We were very pleased with what we accomplished with the program. It was very successful in terms of the positive impact it had on the children and their mothers. It was able to do a lot of activities and have much more impact than we ever dreamed would be possible with the very small amount of money we had available. Here is what the Program Coordinator has to say about what we did:

Box 8.4 The value of using simple puppets with children exposed to violence

When children experience a violent or scary event, they use play and art to work out what they have heard, what they feel, what scares them. They also use it to gain control and feel powerful and strong and try out alternative ways that things can be. Puppets are ideally suited for helping them do this. In addition to being a lot of fun, they provide a structured but open-ended opportunity for children to tell stories about what they know, try out roles, interact with others in a less threatening way than if they took on the roles directly themselves. They also provide adults with a powerful way to safely interact with children around scary events and help children transform their often scary scripts to safer ones. The fact that they can be made simply, with little cost, from simple household materials, make them ideally suited for the play of children in communities affected by violence.

"Well, when I was visiting the project at the beginning, I could hardly find anyone smiling! The children were so depressed that they were not playing. When I go now, it is like a carnival, because all are busy playing in various areas in the room and they have a lot of resources to play with. But remember, the resources were not those that we bought for the project because we did not have a lot of money. These resources are the creation of the program — the teacher, mothers, and children — the things that they were able to create from available resources."

Meeting older children's needs in school

School is supposed to be a safe place for children. If the educational process is going to progress smoothly, safety is a requirement. Unfortunately, in many cases, this has not been the case. For instance, there have been instances when schools themselves got shelled and when children were killed, even inside their classrooms. When this happens, the safety net of the school is broken. And then, just like for the parents, the teachers feel inadequate because they cannot function as the safety valve for the children when they are in school.

To help children deal with the violence in schools, we have added a new role, with the help of Save the Children. That is, in each school there is now what we call the "social counselor." The work of the social counselor is to try to support and advise individual children and families having social or psychosocial problems, especially problems resulting from the violence. In the beginning, social counselors were not trained enough to provide adequate care for the children. And very rapidly, there were too many children who had intense needs for psychological support as a result of exposure to violence. So special programs were developed to provide school counselors with skills and tools to enhance

A kindergarten attacked by missiles in Rafah.

their role as psychosocial supporters to children within the school setting. The training programs were aimed at upgrading school counselors' ability to understand and recognize the psychosocial needs of the children and to be able to provide activities that would increase the children's resilience and improve their coping mechanisms. To achieve these goals, school counselors were trained to use classroom-based interventions and other interventions, such as play therapy activities, that are devoted to improving the pupils' sense of safety and ability to cope.

The programs described above focus on supporting reconciliation and enhancing the mental well-being of children affected by violence. We also felt it was critical to address the deteriorating physical health conditions — such as increasing incidents of malnutrition, anemia, and infections — that resulted from the loss of both physical and financial access to health care. In developing our programs, we took a two-pronged approach. First, we supported the health care system so that the quality of the care provided supports prevention, early detection, and effective management of child illnesses. To do this we focused on improving the community health centers' ability to respond by providing these facilities with the basic infrastructure, equipment, and training for local health workers so they are able to provide quality care.

Second, we provided the primary caretakers at home — mainly mothers — with the information and skills they needed to provide proper care to their children with the aim of reducing, as much as possible, their need to go seek health care that in many cases is inaccessible. To do this, we involved mothers directly in health care programs that promoted the well-being and health of their children.

In Palestine, the four biggest health problems affecting children in the 0-5 year old age group are: diarrhea, respiratory infections, malnutrition, and psychosocial disorders. Therefore, our capacity building program focused on providing caregivers with knowledge and skills to prevent primarily these four diseases, and if prevention does not work, then appropriate home care strategies for treating these children, and only then to seek medical care if all of this was not enough.

Overall, the findings from the evaluation of our health care program convinced us of the value of investing in communities and in the mother. We found that mothers are seeking out less health care because they are taking better care of their kids themselves. They don't need to go out to the city hospital. We are able to help them learn to provide appropriate self-care and to recognize if something is going wrong so they can then move to the service that is in their community. This program is able to demonstrate improvement in the health status indicators such as improved nutritional status of children in the program areas.

Two other significant positive accomplishments of this program were the sustainability of a well-functioning health care system within communities under closures and also the long-term impact it had on empowering women around health issues. We found that our program had given communities the capacity to respond to an emergency themselves. Moreover, by supporting the family to look after themselves after an emergency, the health care system was not over-burdened with children at less risk who could be otherwise well managed at home.

Lessons learned for a better future

In our efforts to protect and promote the well-being of children, several essential principles have guided our efforts. First, as we develop projects that support communities, it is very important that they have clearly stated objectives. Sometimes there may be a need to modify or add to these objectives, but it remains important to keep an eye on the long-term objectives and not to deviate from them even in periods of emergencies. By being focused, I noticed that we not only improved the health outcomes in the communities, but also through creative ways of health education, we created a platform for community activities that brought a lot of joy and happiness to children and their mothers.

Second, all programs addressing the reconciliation and well-being of children should use an empowerment model which builds skills and strengths for dealing with the effects of the conflict in those who are affected by it. This means developing approaches that respect and incorporate the diversity of ideas, abilities, and needs of the program audience.

Finally, it is critical to remember the situation that is creating our need to develop special programs to help children and families cope. It is the "occupation" that stands as the causal factor for all of the issues I have discussed. It is, therefore, through achieving peace that we will ultimately be able to fully address the needs and improve the lives of our children. But until peace is achieved, we have to make loving, caring for, and protecting children our number one priority. They should never be left to suffer or be targeted in political conflict.

Chapter Nine

United States:
Duane Dennis' Story

Although it is the richest industrialized nation in the history of humankind, when compared to other industrialized countries the United States of America ranks 25th in infant mortality; 22nd in low birth rates; 18th in the percentage of children living in poverty; and 13th in the gap between rich and poor children. Additionally, children under 15 in the United States are 12 times as likely to die from gunfire as children in the other 25 industrialized countries combined.

This chapter will focus on children and community violence in the United States. A disproportionate number of children who are affected by violence (as victims and perpetrators), live in the urban areas of the country. These children are also affected by high levels of poverty and racial divisions, the proliferation of gangs and drugs in their communities, and easy access to guns, which are used in the majority of crimes committed in the United States. Children who live in such environments are at risk of abuse, injury, developmental disorders, and long-term mental illness.

Duane Dennis, the Executive Director of Pathways, a community-based organization (CBO) located in central Los Angeles, has been working in early care and education for 18 years. Previously, Dennis was the first Executive Director of the Baltimore City Child Care Resource Center. He began working on violence prevention in some of the most impoverished housing projects in the city of Baltimore, concentrating on interventions for providers, parents, and children.

Estados Unidos
La historia de Duane Dennis

Aun cuando Estados Unidos de América es la nación industrializada mas rica en la historia de la humanidad, cuando se compara con otros países industrializados esta en el puesto numero 25 en cuanto a la tasa de mortalidad infantil; en el lugar 22 en nacimiento de niños con bajo peso al nacer; el puesto numero 18 en el porcentaje de niños/as que viven en situación de pobreza; y el 13 cuando se evalúa la brecha entre los niños/as pobres y ricos. Adicionalmente, niños y niñas menores de 15 años en Estados Unidos, tienen 12 veces más probabilidades de morir por efecto de armas de fuego que los niños y niñas de otros 25 países industrializados de manera combinada.

Este capitulo se enfocara en la violencia en las comunidades y contra los niños y niñas o causada por estos. Un numero desproporcionado de los niños y niñas afectados por la violencia (tanto victimas como victimarios) viven en las áreas urbanas del país. Estos niños también están afectados por altos niveles de pobreza y divisiones raciales, la proliferación de bandas y drogas en sus comunidades, el fácil acceso a armas de fuego, las que son usadas en la mayor parte de los crímenes cometidos en los Estados Unidos. Los niños y niñas que viven en tales ambientes están en riesgo de abuso, de ser heridos, de presentar desordenes en su desarrollo, y desarrollar enfermedades mentales a largo plazo.

Duan Dennos, es Director Ejecutivo de "Pateáis," una organización de base comunitaria (CBO) localizada en Los Angeles, ha estado trabajando en áreas relacionadas con el cuidado y desarrollo infantil temprano durante 18 años. Previamente Dennos fue el primer Director Ejecutivo del Centro de Recursos sobre el Cuidado Infantil de la ciudad de Baltimore. Se inicio trabajando sobre la prevención de la violencia en algunos de los proyectos de vivienda mas pobres de la ciudad de Baltimore, concentrándose en intervenciones dirigidas a proveedores, padres y niños y niñas.

Setting the scene: Violence and inner-city United States

The situation regarding young children and violence in urban areas in the Unites States is a bit different than in most places affected by violence in the rest of the world. There is no internal civil war. There is no war with other countries occurring within our country. The conflict in Iraq does not directly affect most children here. But when you look at children in the United States, especially in our major cities, you are looking at a lot of violence. You are looking at the impact of drugs. There are also high levels of poverty and the impact of the abundance of guns. All of these, separately and combined, have a profound impact on the lives of children and also their families and communities.

There are several issues related to violence that go on for young children who are located in a large United States inner-city like mine. There is a greater degree of crime than in other areas in the country and a greater likelihood for those children to be affected by crime — to see crimes, to be a part of a crime, to see their parents or friends being impacted by crimes. This means that their developmental processes are likely to be somewhat stifled because they are

Box 9.1   Child poverty and its impact in the United States

- Over 13 million children in the United States live below the poverty level.
- Of the 24 million under age 6 in the United States, 21 percent or 5 million live in poor families.
- The research also suggests that there are economic differences by race. For example, while 34 percent of black children and 30 percent of Latino children live in poor families, only 11 percent of white children and 10 percent of Asian children do so.
- Compared to other industrialized countries, the United States ranks: 25th in infant mortality; 13th in the gap between rich and poor children; 22nd in low birth weight rates; and 18th in the percentage of children living in poverty.
- American children under age 15 are 12 times as likely to die from gunfire as children in the 25 other industrialized countries combined.

Source of data: NCCP (2006)

introduced to those conditions that speak to violence, conflict, and disruption at an early age.

Violence and poverty in an urban community: Baltimore

My experiences related to dealing with violence and children really started in inner-city Baltimore in 1990. It was just by chance that I started looking closely at the issue of violence in inner-cities and how children were impacted. I was working in Baltimore as a child care resource and referral (R & R) director. We made links between the parent and child care providers so the parent could make decisions and choose a provider with whom they were comfortable. These child care providers ran small child care programs in their own homes. Unfortunately, there was an unsavory element that knew of the work we were doing and went to providers' homes as parent imposters. What they would do once they got into the home was rob the family child care provider.

We were quite disturbed by what was going on and consequently looked at what we could do to stop it. One of the first things we realized was that we could not deal with the issue independently. If we were going to help prevent family child care providers from being robbed and assaulted, we had to develop some coalitions in the community. With this in mind, we joined forces with the local police department. We had training sessions with family child care providers where we taught them some probing questions to ask if somebody came to their door saying they were referred from the R & R.

Out of that I began asking myself, "What is going on in our community? We have people robbing and victimizing family child care providers — those who are responsible for the upbringing of young children." There was something grossly wrong with that scenario. I decided back then that we needed, as an R & R, to take a stance. We began to develop trainings for providers and young children and their parents on issues of violence.

It soon became broader than just the robbery issue, but that was the trigger. That was the incident that made us pay attention to what young children and families in inner-cities had to deal with. We realized there was a role for the R & R in helping mitigate some of the impact of that violence with parents and work with children. We secured a little funding and began to work with parents, the child care providers, and the children around violence and violence prevention. We really felt that you had to work with all three of them together — the parents, the provider, and the child — for this to work.

Promoting resilience and a sense of safety in children

We developed independent trainings especially for children and their child care providers related to issues of safety and fear. We worked on many practical things. "What do you do if you see a needle on your playground?" This is very common in inner-cities where there are a lot of drugs. One of the things that teachers learned to do, before the children would go onto the playground, was check to make sure that there were no needles or any other dangers to children. "What do you do if you see needles?" and "What do you do if you see somebody with a gun?" We went over the concept of hit the ground and do not run. These were the kinds of practical trainings we developed for our providers and children in child care settings.

We knew there were children at that point who had actually seen guns. For instance, most of the children in the child care centers at housing projects had seen knives and guns. Parents had been victims of violence and there were family members who were perpetrators themselves. Having the ability to address these issues became one of the roles of our R & R. We worked with providers about their own fears, because their abilities to work with children are often impacted by the degree to which they are fearful of the environment and feel that they are susceptible to the same violence that the children are.

A major challenge was giving providers the skills they needed considering their own experiences with violence.

Then the next level was to actually work with parents and children together, because those same children at the centers needed the support to continue when they went home. We wanted to make sure their parents had skills so that they would be able to address their children's fears, too. We know the degree to which we are successful, with regards to the impact of violence, is directly related to the degree that the adults in those children's lives have a positive sense of who they are; and a sense that they are in control and have power to make sure their children can be safe and develop in a healthy way.

Box 9.2   Reducing the impact of violence on children

- A critical factor in determining how violence affects a child, especially at a very young age, is related to caregivers' abilities to cope with their own trauma and grief.

- Many research articles indicate that not all children sustain developmental damage and that there are several factors that contribute to resilience. One factor that research indicates mediates the degree of impact is a secure attachment with a primary caregiver. Parental attention and support is, therefore, extremely important in preventing poor outcomes for children.

Source of information: Berkowitz (2003); NAEYC (2006); and U.S. Department of Health and Human Services (2002). For additional information on U.S. issues see: Garbarino (1999); Garbarino, et al. (1991, 1998); Levin (2003); and Rice & Groves (2006).

Next, my R & R actually wrote a basic paper on this issue primarily using the work of James Garbarino (1999; see also: Garbarino, et al. 1991; 1998). At the time we wrote it, around 1992, it was a really cutting-edge paper for an organization like ours. We were talking about the crucial role of R & Rs and child care providers in reducing the impact of violence on young children and their families. We were asked to present at the National Association for Education of Young Children (NAEYC) annual conference, the biggest early childhood professional organization in the United States. This was when NAEYC was starting to look at the whole issue of violence in children's lives.

Another urban community affected by violence: Los Angeles

My work on young children and violence was placed on hold when I moved to Los Angeles (L.A.) in 1996. But in 2001, the World Forum on Early Care and Education asked me to be on a keynote panel about children, violence, and reconciliation, along with representatives from Israel, Palestine, and Northern Ireland. By that time, I was the Executive Director of Pathways in L.A. It was extraordinary. Even though I was too busy with other business of the agency to focus on violence, the organizers had heard about my work in Baltimore and wanted to have my perspective from the United States along with the other countries that were represented. This whole experience relit the fire, and I started my research again; and as I soon realized, Pathways was the right place to do the work.

Pathways' service area is really diverse, covering a very poor area yet extending to the very affluent Beverly Hills, with everything in between. In addition to helping parents find child care programs for their children, we do a lot of work with children who have special needs. We also distribute the government child care subsidy for our service area;

so as low-income parents are in need of child care we pay providers through the agency. Those were the core services we were doing when I presented at the World Forum on Early Care and Education in Athens. It was during that keynote that I said to myself — the research that I did in Baltimore is very transferable to L.A. Why am I not doing it here? So I began to look at ways Pathways could do the work.

Creating partnerships to better meet children's needs

After my experience with the World Forum, I quickly got Pathways involved, collaborating with several other community organizations in the northeastern part of L.A. — a place called Highland Park — to find ways to respond to the issues of violence in children's lives. This is a high crime, high poverty, and low-income area; and there have been many initiatives there because of the community's vulnerability. Let me just describe what we have been doing there. We have been working with an organization called Hathaway, where one of the collaborators has a Peace Initiative Project. Historically, Hathaway has worked with abused and neglected children. But recently, it has been doing a lot of work in early care and education, believing that this work will reduce the abuse and neglect. They are looking at several issues to make families whole, and they asked us to do the early childhood development piece by training parents and providers. There is a piece in this collaboration that addresses violence. Fortunately or unfortunately, it is less concerned about the child and more concerned about the parent. It works with parents around modeling peaceful behavior for their children and making sure that parents are equipped with tools for being the best possible parents they can be. We have little research thus far; but anecdotally I am seeing parents change their behavior and, therefore, their children are changing.

Another thing we are trying to do now is to look at how we make violence prevention a part of the core work we do in our R & R. I am trying to establish approaches in L.A. that are similar to those developed in Baltimore 10 years ago — a comprehensive approach that is for children, parents, and providers. But, in addition, I've begun really looking at some of the macro issues involved. For instance, the Hathaway project has a very good connection with the police department. We are looking at the gangs in L.A. and why young men choose gangs. We find that those children want what every other child wants. They want to feel supported, they want to feel nurtured, they want to be thought highly of; and they do that through the gangs. If their parents are not able to do this, then the gang becomes, in essence, the surrogate parent. We have, therefore, been looking at alternate ways to meet the same needs; and we are looking at how to intervene with children when they are young, so that they don't go down that path of gangs and violence. For instance, we are trying to develop programs in cooperation with police departments as well as focusing in on pre-teenage children when the gang issue begins. In his books, *Fist, Stick, Knife, Gun* and *Reaching Up to Manhood*, Geoffrey Canada eloquently describes, including from direct experience in his own youth, how street culture in urban areas in the United States can lure boys into a gang culture. He also describes, from his direct experience as a social service professional, how he developed programs for youth that offered them positive ways to meet similar needs to those met by gangs.

One of the Resource and Referral Managers at Pathways is a therapist and an expert on issues related to violence in the home. Although the work we are doing is not directly about domestic violence, we have a lot of domestic violence in our communities; so in our collaboration there is a major mental health component that looks at the psycho-social problems that children deal with as the victims and witnesses of violence. It has a lot of potential to help us develop holistic ways of dealing with families. We think we will be able to find funding to support this effort, always an important consideration in our work. And we are making this a priority.

Consequences of inadequate funding

A lack of adequate funding is having far-reaching implications on what the early childhood community can do to work with children to promote their healthy development in general, including issues around violence. One of Pathways' functions is providing child care subsidies for low-income families. Unfortunately, there are 100,000 children who are on waiting lists for subsidized child care in the County of Los Angeles. There are more eligible children on the waiting lists than there are children being served. This fact has vast implications for the quality of life for the children and their families. And yet the people making the cuts do not seem to think about the far-reaching and long-term effects of what they are doing.

It means there are all kinds of crucial developmental experiences that the excluded children do not get, which undermines their school readiness and preparedness from a social, emotional, and cognitive perspective. This is so important today in those preschool years because there is an ever increasing emphasis in the United States on school readiness and getting children prepared for kindergarten. And, if we do not have well-prepared kindergarteners, there's a chain reaction — they won't be successful in elementary school, middle school, high school, and the likelihood for them to go to college is lessened.

The cuts in subsidies are not just having an impact on children's school readiness. They are affecting the family's fiscal health and economic well-being, the quality of life for people who most need assistance. Parents are more stressed out by the kinds of unsubsidized care they must put their children into because they have to work and provide for their families. This lends itself to a much more stressful situation and higher degrees of stress bring about higher incidences of violence in the children's families. Violence increases at all levels — in the home, in the community, with family members as

Box 9.3 Exposure to violence

At one of the Housing Authority (Public Housing) child care sites in Baltimore City, a trainer encountered two friendly, talkative eight-year-old girls who told of their skill at jumping rope and the rhymes they recited as they jumped. One child recited a "rap" in which the lyrics told of a mother who was on crack, had another baby, and when the social worker came the mommy threw the baby down the garbage chute, and the baby died. And the child related sorely, her big brown eyes shining, "It's true." The trainer, indeed, knew it was true. These children were exposed to a reality that none of us wants to see. Their teachers and caregivers are challenged daily to respond to the child's need to make sense of events that are senselessly cruel and violent.

victims of violence, and as perpetrators. Subsidy dollars for child care are so important in low-income families.

And we are learning more and more about the far-reaching effects violence can have on young children. Over the last 10 years there's a growing body of new research that looks at brain development (see Berkowitz, 2003). The brains of children impacted by violence will develop at much slower rates. I think that's very interesting, because now we understand that there may be some biological issues around children's development. For those children in inner-cities who are constantly being impacted by violence, the evidence now suggests that this is all having a biological effect in slowing down the pace at which their brains may be developing. Their school readiness and all of that comes into play, and their propensity to failure is increasing. I think that is essential to bring into the equation. We really need to have more research around that and take it into account as we work with children. For example, brain research now shows that the developing brain is particularly vulnerable to the impact of violence and that experiences that are overwhelming, frightening, or dangerous can have a toxic effect on the brain. Many neurotransmitters are released at times of fear and anxiety and this can cause abnormalities in the brain during development. As Berkowitz has argued: "This may be one reason why traumatized children have problems learning and integrating new material and data" (Berkowitz, 2003).

Given all of this, it is important to remember that this lack of adequate funds for subsidized spaces is a direct result of the priorities that our government has made with regards to the care of young children. Ironically, it would seem in the United States that as poverty increases and the stakes of the early years get higher, the government tends to abandon its children more and more.

The impact of poverty on the daily life of classrooms

The rising levels of poverty and the reduced resources for child care are directly impacting the children Pathways serves, and this is a big problem. When children living in impoverished situations do not get their basic needs met, the likelihood of those families and children engaging in unproductive behavior increases; and we see this in our preschool programs. We have higher incidences of children who are aggressively acting out, who have behavior issues. When we think of children with special needs (my agency is also a special needs organization), we think of children with increasing medical issues such as: using breathalyzers; being in wheelchairs; and having acute illnesses. However, the majority of special needs children we have are those children who have asthma (which exists at a much higher rate in poor communities) and behavior problems. And in relation to this we are talking about a large number of these children in urban cities in the United States, and a disproportional number of poor urban children are children of color.

Thus far I have not mentioned too much about race. We have considered the issue of poverty and the pathologies that are the result of poverty. We have also considered drugs and proliferation of guns, but we have not focused enough on race. Obviously, race is a major issue when it comes to violence in the United States. We know there are higher incidences of children of color who are impacted by violence. We know there are higher incidences of men of color who actually are in our jails or penal institutions. We also know there are higher incidences of children of color who are a part of gangs.

In addition, there are a disproportionate number of children of color who are impacted by violence and who are also perpetrators of violence and usually end up in our prisons or juvenile institutions. Clearly that suggests something about the future as we are moving forward, with more and more black and brown children occupying our juvenile, special needs, and penal institutions. This means less productivity in our society. We as a society must address the fact that so many children of color are going down those wrong paths and make a commitment to taking the multiple steps that are needed to reverse this inequity, this injustice.

Patterns of aggression at age 8 are highly correlated with patterns of aggression in adulthood (Eron et al., 1994). This means that it is highly likely that many of the older males of color who are involved with violence showed signs of aggression when they were young. Clearly, early care and education has the opportunity to deal with some of that, and I feel those opportunities are when those children are 3 and 4 as opposed to 13 and 14.

Children come to our centers and act out aggression in such severe ways that we cannot handle them. Teachers often have limited training in dealing with aggressive behavior, much less the children with severe behavioral needs. So in addition to trying to provide training on dealing with challenging behavior, we have a program called the Special Needs Advisory Project. It helps providers identify children with special needs — all too often this means

Box 9.4   Race and violence in the United States

The risk of violence is often substantially different for children and youth from different racial and ethnic backgrounds. For example, according to research conducted by Child Trends Data Bank (Brown, et al., 2003):

- Black infants are more than four times as likely as Hispanic and non-Hispanic white infants to be murdered.
- Black teens between the ages of 15 and 19 are nearly twice as likely to be murdered as

Hispanic teens and about 12.5 times as likely to be murdered as non-Hispanic white teens.

As also reported earlier, the National Center for Children in Poverty (NCCP, 2006) reports that:

- The research also suggests that race is related to levels of poverty such that 34 percent of black children and 30 percent of Latino children live in poor families compared to just 11 percent of white children and 10 percent of Asian children.

---

behavior problems. In severe situations this leads to our sending children and their families to mental health professionals. There are also other issues that we identify. For instance, there are children who are non-verbal or who cannot control their bladders, and they are four and five years old. All too often, the children we refer are in critical family situations involving both poverty and violence.

Another issue our child care programs deal with is childhood neglect and abuse. We are mandated by the state to report suspected abuse or neglect, both of which also increase when families are stressed. We conduct training for both our child care center-based staff and our R & R staff. The R & R staff consults with center staff over the phone on decisions about when someone should be referred to the local government agency that deals with abuse and neglect. However, incidences of abuse and neglect are significantly underreported.

Conflicting messages about violence

Not only do we have to be working with children to promote their development and healing, but we also need to know how violence has impacted our own

development as adults. There is a generation of children whose parents have been used to dealing with issues around trouble with violence and going to war. Right now in the United States we get mad at Iraq and so we go and bomb Iraq. So often, what our children are seeing and what we say and do is totally opposite to what adults are trying to teach them. What they are hearing about how grownups function in the world is modeling a culture of violence, at the same time we are trying to teach them violence is wrong. So, we need to think beyond the classroom in our efforts to help children deal with violence and look to the adults, too.

Another place where children learn messages about violence that conflict with what we are trying to teach is from television. They see the news where they see the nation's leaders say violence in war is okay. They see the glorification of violence on programs designed for them as well as on adult programs. And television sets are on in poor homes more than in more affluent homes, and poor children are often supervised less in terms of what they see. We need to help children see grownups promoting peace in their own lives — and in the wider community.

If we want to break the cycle of violence, we can't keep going on with these conflicting messages. It is a generational thing and, therefore, it is going to take time — 15 or 20 years for this generation. So hopefully with quality child care programs that have skills and resources to counteract violence, the 3 and 4 years olds of today won't be the 20 and 21 year olds who will be perpetrators of violence. Then they will grow up to be parents who do not perpetuate the cycle with their parents. But for any of this to happen there has to be resources to help child care and families to succeed. The ideal is to create a community where children's, parents', and the family's needs are being met. We need to work at both the home and child care level. We cannot overemphasize the fact that the degree to which children can deal with conflict is directly related to the adults in their lives. Therefore, working with children and adults in a partnership and realizing that this is a core part of our work is essential for successful outcomes.

Reflecting on a personal journey

My own personal history has played a crucial role in the professional journey I have taken. I grew up in inner-city Baltimore. I have lived in urban areas all my life and have experienced issues around violence. I have had perpetrators and victims in my family and have seen firsthand what certain lifestyles, along with drugs, can do to people, families, and communities. I have also had friends killed because of drugs and drug dealing. Not long before I left Baltimore, a friend of mine and I were talking. He was my very best friend there. We began counting the number of young men who died between the ages of 15 and 30 who were actually friends of mine, childhood playmates, and we counted 17 who had been killed. And it was the result of either a violent death or AIDS.

People often ask me why I did not go that route. I think you get it from your family. In retrospect, when I think about my friends who have been killed — who have been shot or who have died of AIDS — I look at their family structures and what happened in

them. I think it was my parents who were very important in my life. I realize how fortunate I was to have a strong family, to have good models in my life. My father continues to be a very strong figure in my life. It was their focus on issues around limit setting, discipline, and structure and definitely a sense of success through education. I also had uncles and grandparents who always rewarded us for education, if not monetarily, then with a phone call or something to that effect. Education has always been important in my family as an African-American family living in urban Baltimore City. I never thought I was poor when I was young, but in retrospect, when you look at the economic indicators we were poor. Being poor was something that had to do with other people.

Also, I now have a 13-year old African-American son. He has always lived in Baltimore and he goes to public school that does not have the resources it needs and that can be pretty rough. I am always concerned about his well-being, his development, his production, and success in school and in life. So it is just not an issue that is apart from me; it is an issue that is of me. It is not something I can depersonalize because it becomes very personal. And when I think about these issues, I realize my own experiences have a lot to do with why it is so important to me in my work with children today that we also focus on issues of violence and also on families. And it also helps me understand why I get so upset and mad when I see the resources cut that parents need to give their children what they need.

Lessons to share

I often think about how what I have learned from my efforts to help inner-city young children, their families, and child care providers deal with the violence and causes of the violence in children's lives can help others in their efforts. One thing I have learned is that we have to continue focusing on the research piece. Research and evaluation is critical at this particular time; in times of scarcity, we need to know more about which efforts, which interventions can make the biggest difference. I really like what is happening in Northern Ireland as Siobhan and Eleanor describe in their chapter about the work of NIPPA and the *Media Initiative* that is working to reduce sectarian bias from an early age. I like the fact that NIPPA is working with Queen's University Belfast — NIPPA doing the implementation, Queen's doing the evaluation — so they will have a comprehensive evaluation of their efforts that they and others can learn from.

We need to have similar efforts and collaborations in the United States. Doing so will show, from an evaluative standpoint, what happens to young children who are impacted by violence; but more importantly it will show *what* good programs can do as well. We know some of this through the research around Head Start for low-income children in the United States. For instance, we know what has happened developmentally with Head Start children who had positive early care experiences. We need more of this with the things that we are doing now.

I also believe that we need to take very seriously the importance of training child care providers; they provide a potential resource for combating the impact of violence on children that we have only begun to tap. We also still need to work on the attitudes and values of parents, providers, and ourselves because we bring certain biases to the table as it relates to issues around violence. This is especially important with those of us who are of color because it is too easy for us to ask a question like — "If I'm not that way, why do they have to be that way?" And so this whole issue around race discrimination and prejudice comes into play, and we have to figure out how to bring that into our efforts as well.

And finally, we must take seriously the central role early care and education can play as the mitigator between children and violence. After 25 years of doing this work — first being a social worker and then coming into the profession of early childhood education — I believe this now more than ever. While the task before us is difficult, I know it's not impossible.

Chapter Ten

Key Lessons Learned

Reading this book is likely to elicit mixed emotions for many people. Even the briefest attempts at imagining what it must be like to be in a family caught up in violent conflict hurts. It is almost impossible to comprehend just what levels of pain and despair are experienced by young children when they see their parents or their brothers or sisters murdered in front of them or when their families are ripped apart. Some of the symptoms of loss and trauma experienced by children in response to such circumstances — such as repeated nightmares and bedwetting, loss of speech, obsessive attachment to adult family members, and uncontrolled anger — provide just a little insight into the devastating effects that living in a conflict-affected society have on young children.

However, the chapters included in this book are also stories of hope and encouragement. What we have attempted to do through these stories is to show that there are things that we, as early years professionals, can do that can make a real difference. Above all, we

have seen the power that the early years sector can have not only in its ability to provide direct support to children and their families but also in its potential to play an important role more broadly in helping to build peace and foster reconciliation. In this chapter we will focus on drawing out the key lessons learned from the previous chapters and how these might possibly provide a framework of action for others attempting to support children and families in conflict-affected regions.

Before doing this it is useful to draw out from the previous chapters what the key effects of conflict are on children, families, and communities living in conflict-affected societies. This, in turn, will help us to focus on what the nature of the problem is that we as early years professionals need to address. As will be seen, these effects resonate closely with those identified by previous research and outlined in Chapter One. They also give rise to the same six core questions that we posed for ourselves at the end of that chapter.

Lecciones clave aprendidas

La lectura de este libro puede producir emociones encontradas a mucha gente. Aun los menores intentos por imaginar lo que seria formar parte de una familia atrapada en el conflicto, son dolorosos. Es casi imposible comprender los niveles de dolor y

desesperación que experimentan los niños y niñas pequeños cuando ven a sus padres, hermanos o hermanas, asesinados frente a ellos, o cuando sus familias son separadas de manera violenta. Algunos de los traumas o síntomas de perdida experimentados por los niños/as en respuesta a estas circunstancias — tales como las pesadillas constantes; la perdida del habla, el apego obsesivo a los adultos de su familia o la ira incontrolada — nos proporcionan un pequeño "insight" sobre los devastadores efectos que vivir en una sociedad afectada por el conflicto tienen en la temprana infancia.

Sin embargo, los capítulos incluidos en este libro también son historias de esperanza y coraje. Lo que hemos intentado hacer a través de estas historias, es mostrar que hay cosas que los profesionales que trabajan con la niñez temprana podemos hacer para crear una diferencia real. Sobre todo, hemos visto el poder que el sector de la infancia tiene, no solo para proporcionar apoyo directo a los niños, niñas y sus familias, sino también en su potencial para jugar un rol más amplio muy importante, ayudando a la construcción de la paz y la reconciliación. En este capitulo nos enfocaremos en el desarrollo de las lecciones mas importantes aprendidas de los

capítulos previos. Y en como pueden estas lecciones proveer un marco de acción para otros que intentan apoyar las familias, los niños y niñas, en regiones afectadas por el conflicto armado.

Antes de hacer esto es útil extraer de los capítulos precedentes cuales son los principales efectos del conflicto sobre la niñez, las familias y las comunidades que viven en sociedades afectadas por el conflicto. Esto a su vez, nos ayudara a enfocarnos en la naturaleza del problema que tendremos que afrontar como profesionales trabajando con la temprana infancia. Como se vera, estos efectos se aproximan mucho a aquellos identificados por investigaciones previas que han sido descritos en el primer capitulo. También apoyan las mismas seis preguntas centrales que propusimos la finalizar ese primer capitulo.

The effects of conflict on children, families, and communities

One of the key points to emerge from the previous chapters is that each conflict situation is unique and the violence associated with it manifests itself in different ways. In Albania, for example, there are the "blood feuds" while in Colombia there is the high incidence of kidnapping for ransom or revenge. Similarly, Nepal has experienced high level of child abductions, often with the aim of political indoctrination, while Bosnia and Herzegovina is now emerging from an intense and violent period of ethnic cleansing. In Chad there is the acute problem of absolute poverty fueling existing tensions and conflict, while in the United States communities are being ripped apart by gun crime and drugs. Moreover, segregation and deep social divisions tend to underpin a number of conflict-affected regions. This can be seen for example, in relation to Palestine where certain communities are physically isolated and feel "under siege." However, even in societies

emerging from conflict and attempting to build peace, such as the case with Northern Ireland, the legacy of those divisions remain.

What is perhaps most remarkable from the stories recounted from all of these regions is the fact that the fundamental issues facing those working with young children and their families are so similar. Regardless of the nature and type of conflict that exists, three central issues tend to emerge through all of the stories to one degree or another, and we will look briefly at each in turn.

The direct effects of conflict on young children

First, while the nature and scale of the violence has differed from one situation to the next, the fact remains that in all of these places children have not only been the direct casualties of conflict but have also suffered physically and emotionally from being caught up in and witnessing violent events. Not surprisingly, therefore, all of the stories recounted in previous chapters point to the many children who have been left traumatized by seeing their own family members murdered, raped, or tortured as well as having to live under a cloud of fear. This cloud of fear can often be intensified for children exposed to television and radio news reporting that act as constant reminders of the threat out there.

Moreover, another theme running through these chapters has been the lack of opportunity that children have to explore and express their feelings. Many of the chapters, for example, have drawn attention to the lack of a safe space for children to begin to come to terms with their experiences and the attitudes they are beginning to develop from these. In addition there has often been an understandable reluctance on the part of early years educators and parents to even begin examining all of this with their children. After all, they are as much victims of the conflict as the children are and so will often find it an issue that is incredibly difficult and painful to deal with. As we have seen, what this often leads to is a situation where children tend to be left to their own devices to try to make sense of what is happening around them. For some, the gravity of the situation simply leads to post-traumatic stress as described above. For others, and as reported in several chapters, children will do their best to try to understand what is happening to them through re-enacting through their play the violent events and fighting they have witnessed. Not surprisingly, with little guidance or support, children will have little opportunity other than to develop partial and distorted world views where violence and division are normalized. This, in turn, can help to fuel conflict for the next generation.

Given these experiences, we are left with two key questions for those working with children and families in conflict-affected societies as originally posed at the end of Chapter One:

- What support can we give to caregivers in helping them deal with the effects of violence in their children's lives?
- How can we best listen to the voices of young children and help them to explore, in a safe

environment, their experiences of conflict and the beliefs, fears, and anxieties that arise from these?

The effects of conflict on families

The second key theme underpinning the stories recounted in previous chapters is the effect that conflict has on families. Many families are left to deal with the trauma and loss associated with family members who have been killed or have simply disappeared. Moreover, there can be significant adjustments required in families where one or more of their members have been injured as a result of being caught up in the conflict. All of this can place considerable strain and stress on families that, in turn, is often picked up and internalized by the children.

This, however, is only part of the picture. We have seen that conflict often leads to the loss of male family members, in particular, who tend either to be the targets of warring factions or who are drawn directly into the conflict themselves. As found in relation to the stories from Albania and Nepal, for example, this can often lead to families without any adult males. Not only are there no male role models for the children, but this can place additional pressure on families as they struggle to survive having much less capacity to earn a living.

In addition, we have seen recent examples from Bosnia and Herzegovina, Colombia, Chad, Nepal, and Palestine of large numbers of families being displaced as a result of conflict. Even in post-conflict societies such as Northern Ireland, while the scale of such displacement is now much less, there are still occasions where families are burned out of their own homes or forced to flee for their own safety. As reported in several chapters, this in turn can often place such families in extremely vulnerable positions; often being unable to find work and so being plunged into poverty and ill-health. We have also seen reports of children of displaced families being unable to attend school or facing difficulties when attending new schools. For many families, even when the conflict has ended, as in Bosnia and Herzegovina and Nepal, there is a strong reluctance to return to their home town or village because of the trust that has been broken. For some they are thus condemned to an immediate future where they are not only vulnerable economically and in terms of their health and general well-being, but they are also suffering from detachment from and thus loss of their fundamental sense of cultural identity and belonging.

There are also examples from all of the stories reported in the previous chapters of families completely disintegrating as a result of killings, displacement, and/or being ripped apart as individual members flee for their own safety. Such experiences have been recounted to one degree or another in all of the stories included in this book and lead us, as early years professionals, back to two further questions originally posed in Chapter One:

- In situations where there are high and intense levels of violence, how do we go about meeting the needs of children when their families and communities are literally disintegrating?
- How can we begin to work effectively with families and communities in the many different contexts created by political violence and armed conflict?

The effects of conflict on wider communities

Finally, and as we have seen, it is not just families that are destroyed by conflict but also whole communities. Communities can often be found to literally disintegrate as families are forced to flee for fear of their lives. Moreover, in the throes of conflict the very basic infrastructure of communities can be destroyed as opposing factions purposely target hospitals, roads, sanitation, and water supplies. In Bosnia and Herzegovina, Nepal, and Palestine, for example, we have seen stories of schools and nurseries either being targeted for attack or taken over by military forces.

Such forms of conflict do not just lead to significant numbers of people being displaced but can also lead to the creation of new, and deeply divided communities where the legacy of such divisions — as in Bosnia and Hervegovina and Northern Ireland — can continue for generations. Moreover, conflict not only leads to divisions between communities but can also create divisions within communities. As seen from the stories recounted from Colombia and the United States, whole communities can begin to disintegrate from within as a result of violence and crime.

Being an integral part of the community, the early years sector cannot avoid these wider effects of the conflict on their communities. Alongside providing direct support to children and families we therefore need to look beyond this and ask ourselves two final questions, again as posed originally at the end of Chapter One:

- How can we be effective advocates for children living in conflict-affected societies?
- What role can we, as early years professionals, play in terms of helping to build the peace?

Key lessons learned

This, then, is the nature of the problem faced by early years professionals working in conflict-affected societies. As encapsulated by the six core questions, it is a problem that is multi-layered and therefore requires a multi-layered response. Not only do we need to continue to work directly with children and families, we also need to engage effectively with the wider community and also, beyond this, to develop a more strategic and advocacy-based role.

Fortunately, there is a wealth of experience contained in the preceding chapters that we can learn from. In particular, there are seven key lessons that can be drawn out that may be useful to other early years professionals working in conflict-affected societies. Each will now be explained in turn but, in summary, they are:

1. There is a need to develop quality, child-centered environments for young children.

2. There is a need to create safe spaces for children to express and explore their feelings, including those related to their experiences of the conflict.

3. There is a need to provide training and ongoing support to those working with young children and families.

4. There is a need to provide direct support to parents.

5. There is a need to adopt a community development approach that aims to empower local communities and build capacity so that they can develop and maintain early years services for themselves.

6. The early years sector has considerable potential to contribute to peace building and reconciliation more broadly.

7. The early years sector has an important role to play nationally and internationally in advocating for children and bringing pressure to bear for peace.

It is important to stress that these lessons should not be treated as a complete and comprehensive list of "what to do." There is still so much more that we need to learn and share internationally as will be described in the next chapter. However, these lessons learned do provide a clear outline of some of the approaches we feel have been important and have worked for us. Moreover, we have confidence in these precisely because they resonate closely with our experiences drawn from working in many different conflict-affected societies and regions.

For the sake of clarity, we have organized the lessons learned under three headings: those related to working directly with children and families; those related to working with the wider community; and finally, those related to working more strategically

towards bringing about longer-term change. However, while reported in this way, it is important to stress that they are all inter-related. It is the active combination of all of these lessons learned that we feel begins to create an agenda for the early years sector in conflict-affected societies.

Working directly with children and families

In terms of working directly with children and families, four key lessons have emerged from the previous chapters.

1. There is a need to develop quality, child-centered environments for young children.

A concern shared by all of those whose stories have been shared in previous chapters is the need to create a quality early education and care environment for young children that is child-centered and culturally and developmentally appropriate. Young children, therefore, need to be given the opportunity to explore their surroundings, develop social and emotional competence, and express themselves in a wide range of differing ways. Moreover, we as adults need to be able to listen and understand children through the many different ways they choose to express their feelings and perspectives. This is the foundation stone that then creates an environment that makes it possible for children to explore and work through the violence and events they see happening around them (see Lesson 2).

In many respects, transforming an early years setting into one that is child-centered does not require significant resources but can often be achieved by making use of existing resources and materials that are around. In Albania, for example, where many of the settings are based in rural areas, they found it possible to make use of the wealth of natural resources that surrounded them including leaves, conkers, fir cones, and twigs to make collages, models, and pictures.

Moreover, and as illustrated by the story from Bosnia and Herzegovina, it is important not just to uncritically accept and apply "quality standards" from elsewhere but to explore and adapt them to the specific contexts within which a particular setting is located. This in turn requires a wider community development model where early years professionals, parents, and the wider community are involved in developing and delivering early years services (see Lesson 5). In fact this, itself, is dependent upon those involved having the capacity to contribute meaningfully to this process (see Lessons 3 and 4) and whereby strong and effective networks are created among all those involved as a result (see Lesson 5).

2. There is a need to create safe spaces for children to express and explore their feelings, including those related to their experiences of the conflict.

It is only through creating child-centered environments for children that we can begin to support children in terms of providing them with the space to make sense of their experiences and to express and explore their feelings. Clearly, this requires the creation of "safe spaces" where children feel physically and emotionally safe and thus have the confidence to be able to begin expressing themselves. As we have seen, simply creating this safe space can be extremely difficult, especially in areas where conflict is ongoing. However, as the stories from Palestine and Northern Ireland have shown, this is possible. Moreover, even where children's spaces are being routinely targeted and used by warring factions, the example from Nepal and the success of the Children as Zones of Peace campaign shows that through collective action and advocacy it is possible to challenge this (see Lesson 7).

Within these safe spaces it is important to provide children with the opportunity to discuss and explore their experiences of the conflict if they wish to and to express their feelings about this. At one level this can be done with the use of existing resources available in a child-centered environment (Lesson 1) as well as

the creation of other inexpensive materials, such as puppets as discussed in the story from Palestine. However, and at another level, this does rely upon the adults in those settings having the skills to be able to support and encourage the children effectively, which as already noted is not always easy when they may have been affected by the conflict themselves. As such this does require significant investment in terms of the training and ongoing support of those working with young children (see Lesson 3).

3. There is a need to provide training and ongoing support to those working with young children and families.

Given some of the situations described in previous chapters, it is not surprising to find that in some situations the struggle is simply to create a safe and dedicated space for children. However, for that space to be effective it needs to be child-centered, as already argued; and this, in turn, requires adults who have the knowledge and skills to create and maintain this effectively. This, however, does not just require training in relation to such core matters as child development, children's rights, and child-centered care and education. When dealing with the effects of conflict among children and families, it also requires a whole set of additional skills. In situations where everyone is affected by conflict to one degree or another, an essential part of this includes providing early years professionals with the skills necessary to be able to identify and reflect upon their own experiences, attitudes, and prejudices. As illustrated by the stories from Northern Ireland and also Bosnia and Herzegovina, training is needed that encourages self-exploration and open, honest, and respectful dialogue among those involved.

Beyond this there is also the need to provide training for those working directly with children and families in terms of how they can most effectively deal with issues raised around the conflict. As the work reported in the story from Northern Ireland has shown, this involves not only dealing with the fears and anxieties that parents may have but also how to respond to the negative attitudes and prejudices that young children themselves might raise, and thus to promote understanding of and respect for diversity.

4. *There is a need to provide direct support to parents.*

From the last example it can be seen that for any approach to be effective there is a need to work in partnership with parents. As we have seen, this has been a strong theme running through all of the chapters. It certainly involves increasing the awareness of parents about key issues relating to early child care and development, including issues relating to health care as reported in the story from Palestine and around issues of fear and personal safety as covered in the story from the United States. Crucially, it also involves reaching out to and involving fathers as well as mothers as shown in relation to Albania.

Beyond this there is a need to provide parents with the training to be able to provide their children with the help and support they need in relation to the conflict. In Colombia, for example, this has included providing training to parents on how they can use drama and art as ways of helping their children work through the stress and trauma they may be experiencing. In addition, there is a need to ensure that there is continuity between the approach taken in the early years setting and what goes on at home. As shown in Northern Ireland, this can involve the creation of simple resources that children make and/or play with in the setting but then take home to encourage further exploration with their parents.

Working with the wider community

As already indicated through the discussion above, creating child-centered environments and working effectively with children and families require a broader community development approach. It is only through involving the communities themselves and providing them with the capacity to create and maintain early years settings that any initiatives will be effective and sustainable. This recognition, in turn, leads onto the next two lessons learned from the experiences recounted in the previous chapters.

5. *There is a need to adopt a community development approach that aims to empower local communities and build capacity so that they can develop and maintain early years services for themselves.*

There is certainly nothing wrong with outside agencies providing support to local communities to help meet the needs of their children and families. However, for this to be effective it needs to work from where the community is at, and aim to give them ownership of any services that are put in place, and also to develop their capacity to be able to run and sustain these in the longer-term. The problems of outside agencies coming into a region with a pre-determined response and set of services that bear little relationship to the needs of local communities and families was illustrated by the story from Bosnia and Herzegovina.

However, this need not be the case. The example of the work of the Christian Children's Fund (CCF) in Albania shows how it is possible for outside agencies to work effectively to support local communities by employing local people, conducting comprehensive needs assessments, and giving local communities ownership of the services that are developed. As stressed in relation to the story from Chad, communities will only effectively begin to heal when they have opportunities to help themselves. For this type of community development approach to be effective, there needs to be a concerted effort at bringing key organizations and agencies together to create strategic networks. This was one of the key messages to emerge from the story recounted from the United States, where effective community coalitions had to be built to begin addressing crime and violence within communities. CINDE's Family and Community Centers, described in the story from Colombia, provide another example of the effectiveness of creating local networks to help share experiences and resources, as does the national network of organizations that the Resource Center described in the story from Nepal has established.

Within this, there is a need to be strategic and thus set clear objectives in relation to the networks that are to be established. This is a point made strongly by Ali Shaar from his experience in Palestine. It is also a point illustrated by the establishment of the *Media Initiative for Children* — Northern Ireland where very clear and achievable goals were essential to the success of the program. Indeed, this last example also illustrates the positive role that outside agencies can play — in this case the US-based Peace Initiatives Institute — in encouraging and facilitating that type of networking. However, within all of this there is a need to ensure that local organizations have the resources as well as the capacity to enable them to network and participate as equals within a partnership.

Finally, another important strand found in relation to this type of community development approach is the need to develop effective and visionary leaders from within the early years sector. This can be seen, for example, in relation to the innovative educational programs described in the story from Colombia where CINDE has developed strong partnerships with a number of local universities to provide high quality postgraduate training — up to and including Ph.Ds — to help equip the existing and next generation of leaders.

6. The early years sector has considerable potential to contribute to peace building and reconciliation more broadly.

There is no doubt that the early years sector has so much potential to be a power for good in regions affected by conflict. As already stressed, through the provision of high quality child care and education, it is possible to set the foundations upon which future generations can emerge who are confident, secure, and socially aware and who also respect cultural differences and are inclusive in their outlook. However, this is only part of the picture. Through adopting the type of community development approach outlined above, the early years sector also has the potential to make an important contribution to building the peace more generally within and between existing communities. More specifically, there is something about early childhood that can transcend existing political divides and encourage those involved in conflict to re-focus their attention and priorities and to think instead of their own children and their future.

One example of the power of the early years was provided by the story from Albania. While in many ways Albania is a traditional and patriarchal society, the work of the early years sector there has not just encouraged men to be more involved in the care of their children; but, crucially, it has also provided the stepping stone from which it has been possible to begin engaging some of the men in conflict resolution work. Given the deeply-entrenched nature of the conflict in Albania, organized as it is around blood feuds, it is difficult to see how this may have been achieved other than through building upon the men's genuine concerns for their children and grandchildren and their futures.

Similarly, the story from Chad has shown how efforts to develop effective early childhood centers provided the basis from which broader issues, in this case gender inequalities, could begin to be dealt with and overcome. Moreover, in societies that remain deeply-divided, it has been shown how a focus on the early years has helped to provide shared spaces where caregivers from both sides of the divide are able to come together to share experiences and perspectives and to provide mutual support. As recounted in the story from Northern Ireland, this was possible even during the height of the conflict here. Nowadays, in Northern Ireland and other societies emerging from conflict, such as Bosnia and Herzegovina, the early years sector is playing an important role in drawing divided communities together and building peace.

Perhaps the key point underpinning all of this, however, is the need to begin from where communities are at and to identify and address the real needs that children and families in those communities have. It is only through this that genuine trust and effective relationships can be built that will, in turn, allow other peace-building goals to be set and addressed. It is therefore important not to begin by attempting to impose different values and beliefs on communities. As the experience from Albania showed, significant change in the behaviour of men towards child care and towards violence is now beginning to be achieved precisely because the initial focus was on building up trust and confidence through providing quality early childhood environments, rather than beginning with an explicit and political stance regarding gender equality.

Working towards longer-term change

Ultimately, there is a need to be realistic. Each of the conflicts described in the foregoing chapters has its own economic and political roots and, ultimately, will only ever be effectively resolved through economic and political means. The early years sector cannot, therefore, bring an end to conflict and build peace in and of itself. However, and as with every other sector within a society affected by conflict, it has a role to play. For the early years sector, we have set out what some of this role might be above as drawn out from the proceeding chapters.

Much of the role set out so far has been concerned with working directly with local communities to meet the needs of children and families. There is, however, a wider role that the early years sector can play

nationally and internationally in terms of advocating for children and thus bringing political pressure to bear in regions affected by conflict, and this brings us to our last key lesson.

7. *The early years sector has an important role to play nationally and internationally in advocating for children and bringing pressure to bear for peace.*

As mentioned earlier, it is one thing to recommend the creation of safe areas for children and yet entirely another thing to actually create these, especially in societies riven by conflict. What the example from Nepal of the Children as a Zone of Peace campaign has shown is the power that a wider advocacy campaign can have in bringing about change. As already mentioned, one of the features of the conflict in Nepal was the targeting and use of schools by opposing forces as well as the significant numbers of children being abducted for the purposes of political indoctrination. Through the effective use of the news media and a coordinated awareness campaign, a coalition of organizations was able to get all sides to commit themselves to a 10-point plan to avoid children being exposed to or drawn into the conflict.

Part of the success of this campaign has undoubtedly been the fact that the concern for the safety and well-being of children was shared by all parties involved. It is in this sense that the power of early childhood can be seen in its ability to transcend political divides. However, the success of the campaign was also related to the ability of the news media to provide "hard evidence" of the effects of the conflict on children. This, in turn, points towards the important role that research can play in advocacy work by providing evidence of the plight of children and the effects that conflict is having on their lives and those of their families. Moreover, research can also play a key role in evaluating the effectiveness of particular initiatives, as illustrated by the story from Northern Ireland, as well as being used as a resource for others to draw upon as described by the story from Nepal.

Of course early years professionals can also conduct their own research into the needs of the children and families they work with, as well as into the effectiveness of the programs and services they deliver. What this brings us back to is the importance of training and capacity building and the role that universities can play, not only in undertaking research directly, but also in building research capacity among the early years sector more widely.

Conclusions

What we have tried to do in this chapter is to draw out the key lessons learned from the stories told in the previous chapters. While these stories have been difficult to read at times because of the pain and suffering they have recounted, it is also important to recognize that these are stories of hope and encouragement as well. While conflict is brutal and can create appalling situations that children and families find themselves in, there is plenty of evidence provided in this book that there is

something that the early years sector can do about this.

In this chapter we have attempted to identify and draw out the key lessons learned from across the different stories. As shown, while each conflict situation is unique, the key issues that arise for children and families is remarkably similar. This, in turn, has enabled us to draw out seven key lessons, as outlined above, that are sufficiently generic to be applicable to a wide range of conflict-affected societies. As we have seen, these lessons have included the need for training and capacity building and for approaches based upon community development models. They have also focused on the need for strategic networking, at all levels, as well as strong advocacy work at national and international levels and applied research to support this.

These key lessons, in turn, provide a natural starting point for the final chapter which describes the development, current work, and future plans of the International Working Group on Peace Building with Young Children. It is, therefore, to this that the book now turns.

Chapter Eleven

Ways Forward:
The International Working Group on
Peace Building with Young Children

This book has presented the stories of a range of people working with young children and caregivers in areas affected by conflict. Through their experiences and perspectives we have found that, while each situation is unique, there are still a number of underlying issues and lessons to be drawn that are common to all contexts to varying degrees. These key lessons were drawn out in the last chapter. The purpose of this final chapter is to explore possible ways forward. In particular, the chapter describes the development, current work, and future plans of the International Working Group on Peace Building with Young Children. It tells the story of how a loosely connected group of individuals who were working with young children and their families in regions experiencing or emerging from conflict turned into a force reaching beyond local, regional, and national boundaries. The chapter identifies the key process steps that underpinned the successful formation of the International Working Group and then describes the current aims and objectives of the International Working Group and its future plans to support the early childhood sector and address the key lessons identified in the last chapter.

Vías para Avanzar: El Grupo Internacional de Trabajo en Pacificación con Niños Pequeños

Este libro ha presentado historias de una variedad de personas que trabajan con niños y niñas pequeños en áreas afectadas por el conflicto. A través de sus experiencias y perspectivas hemos encontrado que, aun cuando cada situación es única, hay un número de asuntos subyacentes y de lecciones que pueden extraerse como comunes a todos los contextos, aun cuando en diferentes grados.

Estas lecciones se describen en este capitulo final. El propósito del capitulo es explorar caminos posibles. En particular, se describe el desarrollo, trabajo actual, y los planes futuros del Grupo Internacional de Trabajo sobre Construcción de Paz con la Temprana Infancia. En este capitulo se cuenta la historia de cómo un grupo de individuos conectados muy someramente, quienes estaban trabajando con niños pequeños y sus familias en regiones que experimentan conflicto emergente, se ha convertido en una fuerza con mayor alcance, mas allá de las fronteras locales, nacionales o regionales. El capitulo identifica los pasos claves en el proceso, que subyacen a la conformación exitosa del Grupo de Trabajo, y sus planes futuros para apoyar el sector de la temprana infancia y para responder a los asuntos centrales identificados.

Early childhood professionals working together

The formation and work of the International Working Group on Peace Building with Young Children is the story of how a loosely connected group of individuals, whose common issues may not have been immediately apparent, turned into a force reaching beyond local, regional, and national boundaries. The group supported and sustained each other, developed this book and have long-term plans to continue to raise awareness and to make a difference. While the idea of bringing together professionals to identify common concerns, issues, and strategies is not a particularly unusual notion, the way in which the International Working Group developed and crystallized is worth reviewing as it does reflect a relatively unique approach within the early childhood sector to addressing the needs of young children and their caregivers living in conflict-affected societies on a truly global scale.

The International Working Group represents the first of several projects conceived by the World Forum Foundation and has achieved some important and successful outcomes. Within this it is possible to identify a number of key steps in the process of its development that have helped the International Working Group achieve some of its most important goals. These steps are described below in the hope of inspiring others to develop their own approaches to developing information and support networks. The chapter concludes with an outline of the current structure and plans for the International Working Group and details of where you can find more information.

Key process steps in establishing the working group

In 2004 The World Forum Foundation in partnership with NIPPA — The Early Years Organisation —

Box 11.1 Comments from delegates at the Working Forum Belfast conference on "Building Bridges: Healing Communities through Early Childhood Education," November 17-20, 2004

"Understand each other, work with each other, involve parents and communities, build on strengths, and remember what you have in common rather than what you don't."

"We are all from different backgrounds, cultures, and have different historical experiences, but we have one common goal: to ensure that all children's experiences are positive and beneficial to their growth and development."

"I see now that it is possible for troubled and divided communities to heal themselves through young children."

organised the first "Working Forum." The theme was "Building Bridges: Healing Communities through Early Childhood Education." The organisers, Bonnie and Roger Neugebauer of the World Forum Foundation and Siobhan Fitzpatrick and her team at NIPPA, conceived the original idea to bring together a group of practitioners, researchers, and others who were working with young children in conflict and post-conflict areas. These participants, and a few more, became the International Working Group (see Box 11.2).

Below, we describe the steps towards the realization of our group as an effective and sustainable entity.

Step 1:
Defining the goal

For the International Working Group the aim was to create a meeting place for awareness raising, discussion, and debate around the issue of children affected by conflict. With this in mind, the initial goal of the International Working Group was to identify early childhood professionals doing important and innovative work in conflict-affected societies and to facilitate the sharing of their experiences and perspectives so that lessons could be learned regarding the nature of the issues and challenges they face and examples of good practice could be drawn out and disseminated. In bringing early childhood professionals with a common focus together in one place, it was anticipated that similarities could be identified and explored. The outcome, it was hoped, would be an articulation of the achievements and potential for early childhood professionals to act as agents for peace and reconciliation that would, in turn, resonate with others around the globe and in this way support all those who are dealing with the devastating outcomes of children caught in conflict situations.

Step 2:
Identifying the participants

For the International Working Group, participants were identified through personal networks and the recommendations of others to reflect experiences, regional representation and a variety of perspectives.

Box 11.2 International Working Group on Peace Building with Young Children

This listing reflects the groups as organized for Working Forum Belfast and the creation of this book.

Authors
- Paul Connolly, Northern Ireland
- Jacqueline Hayden, Australia
- Diane Levin, United States

Organising Team
- Bonnie Neugebauer, World Forum Foundation, United States
- Roger Neugebauer, World Forum Foundation, United States
- Siobhan Fitzpatrick, NIPPA, Northern Ireland
- Pauline Walmsley, NIPPA, Northern Ireland

Rapporteurs
- Jacqueline Hayden, Australia
- Isobel McClean, Northern Ireland
- Janet Preston, Northern Ireland
- Ena Shaw, Northern Ireland
- Lisa Ruth Shulman, United States
- Agatha Thapa, Nepal
- Kathryn Weill, United States
- Samantha Kettyle, Northern Ireland

Working Team Facilitators
- Betty Burkes, United States
- Diane Levin, United States

Working Team Participants
- Marta Arango, Colombia
- Paul Connolly, Northern Ireland
- N. Urbain Dembélé, Mali
- Duane C. Dennis, United States
- Andrew Ikupu, Papua New Guinea
- Ingrid Jones, Albania
- Eleanor Mearns, Northern Ireland
- Ayshe Najjar, Israel
- Félicien Ntakiyimana, Chad
- Elisa del Puerto, Philippines
- Radmila Rangelov-Jusović, Bosnia and Herzegovina
- Norma Rudolph, South Africa
- Ali Shaar, Palestine
- Kishor Shrestha, Nepal
- Aleksandra Selak Zivkovic, Croatia

Each participant was to have experience in working with children, families, and/or communities from conflict-ridden, violent, and other disruptive environments. However, despite attempts to ensure geographical representation and a spread of interests, some of the nominated participants were unable to join. Other participants ended up in the group because of serendipitous reasons. Strangely, this did not seem to matter and through the way the International Working Group was organised (see Steps 3 to 6 below) it coalesced perfectly. One of the lessons learned from this process was that it is less important to have members of the International Working Group representing specific roles, as it is to ensure that processes involved can make use of, and build upon, the strengths and knowledge base that each individual has to offer.

Step 3:
Pre-meeting preparation

Once the list of participants had been confirmed, an eList (electronic mailing list) was established and circulated to all. This allowed the participants to communicate with each other; and the facilitators began the process of introductions and team development using this medium. Each participant was invited to participate in this several months in advance. The purpose was clearly articulated with each participant sharing the experiences, major concerns, and successes related to their own situation. Guiding questions were distributed using the listserv to assist with reflection and preparation. This pre-meeting activity clarified the goals for participants and allowed them to gather information within their regions, where necessary. All of this contributed to the efficiency and effectiveness of the face-to-face meeting time, and became a facet of each subsequent meeting.

Step 4:
Including informal time and "trust building" activities from the outset

When participants first met, they took part in a range of informal activities such as sharing meals, telling stories, and discussing their individual goals and hopes for the meeting, before actually getting down to "business." The informal time facilitated the development of trust, which allowed group members to discuss sensitive issues and topics. One particularly powerful activity was the "Appreciation Table." Here each participant was asked to place an object of personal significance to themselves on the table and then given a few minutes to tell why they had chosen that object. The exercise provided an opportunity for everyone to share information about their concern for their region in a very personal way. International Working Group members immediately felt the bonds and mutual support which developed from this simple exercise.

Step 5:
Structuring the context and the processes

Participation in the International Working Group was categorised according to three distinct roles. The first consisted of the participants themselves who represented front line workers dealing with the effects of conflict on young children and families on a daily basis. This number was kept small (12-15), and this allowed people to sit in a circle during group to ensure eye contact and ease of interaction. A second role within the group was that of rapporteur. This consisted of a small team who did not actively participate in the discussions but made notes on important points, delineated issues which needed clarification, and provided a summary at the end of each session. Rapporteurs had diverse experience in the area of children and conflict. Collectively, they represented many perspectives. This was deemed to be a significant factor in the success of this team. The rapporteurs sat in an outer circle around the participants.

The third function consisted of facilitation. Two expert facilitators — Betty Burkes and Diane Levin — developed each day's agenda and ensured that discussions stayed focused and relevant. The facilitators also ensured that all participants had equal chances to speak. This was especially important for the International Working Group because a number of participants were working in a second language.

Step 6:
Sharing ideas and perspectives

Participants were given a set period of time to tell about the situations and issues within their geographical regions. Some participants had prepared audio/visual presentations. Others presented with narratives and stories. While some instructions had been given, the framework was loose enough for each participant to share their story in a way that was comfortable for them. By the end of the first day, all participants agreed that despite the overarching goal of identifying similarities, it was critical that the unique characteristics of each conflict and post-conflict situation be acknowledged and respected. Beyond the search for generalized issues, the group focused upon identifying ways in which the early childhood sector can support and empower communities to address their individual (contextually relevant) strategies for peace.

Step 7:
Articulating and disseminating the outcome of group meetings

We believe that the International Working Group has a responsibility to include broad participation and to stimulate discussion and debate as it works towards its stated goals. The incorporation of ways to interact with an appropriate "audience" will keep the group grounded and relevant. In our case the International Working Group was tied to the delivery of an early childhood conference in Belfast. Over 250 delegates had signed on for presentations and workshops on peace and reconciliation. The International Working Group had been named as the main speakers for this event. This slightly pressured need for the International Working Group to report in public had two results. First, it ensured that the team stayed focused and helped the International Working Group to articulate messages in a clear way that could resonate with a wide audience. Second, the public presentations stimulated debate and discussions and appreciation from the delegates. This, in turn, had the result of helping the International Working Group to note the importance of their work and re-motivated them to continue to work towards their goals.

For the conference, the International Working Group broke into three panels based on three major themes. These were:

- The nature of conflicts in the world: information about the diversity of conflict situations related to children, families, and communities

- The impact of conflicts on children, families, communities and the resulting needs of children

- Reconciliation programs, approaches, and strategies within early childhood programs in response to conflict.

Following each panel presentation, conference delegates met in designated discussion groups. Discussion Group Leaders had been recruited to facilitate these meetings and draw out the learning and issues from each group. The reporting from these discussions has played a key role in influencing the development of this book.

Another way to spread the word took place during field trips to programs and projects across Northern Ireland. These trips allowed members of the International Working Group to interact with the conference delegates over long time periods. The informal discussions which took place on that day enriched the work of both participants. The trips also allowed parties to become aware of situations and issues in the host country while child care specialists within the country were given the opportunity to interact with the international participants and delegates. Some excellent sharing ensued.

Step 8:
Reaching closure and preparing for the next steps

The first meeting of the International Working Group closed with a final opportunity to recap on the processes, the experiences, the learnings, and the new questions which were raised. The final step was to determine how to ensure that none of this was lost. A team took on a coordination role to ensure that the work would be built upon. This book is one direct outcome of the International Working Group. The group also felt that it was important to commit to meeting again in May 2005 at the World Forum for Care and Early Education in Montreal, Quebec, Canada. This further meeting was important in terms of setting goals for the group, providing an opportunity for visibility within the sector, and continuing to build relations within the group.

Beyond meeting in Montreal in May 2005, the International Working Group also met in Manizales, Colombia in May 2006. A number of individuals in the group have also exchanged visits and/or assisted each other with particular projects. The meeting in Manizales was particularly important in focusing on defining the focus, mission, goals, processes, and work program for the group in line with the key lessons identified through this book. The meeting gave attention to the importance of hearing the voice of young children in regions experiencing or emerging from conflict, and participants exchanged ideas and strategies for doing so. The Manizales meeting also focused on professional development and partnerships between universities and civil society organisations to develop specific learning and development programs for early childhood professionals working in these regions. The

first of these programs, the postgraduate MSc in Social Inclusion and the Early Years will be available through Queen's University Belfast from September 2007.

Future plans

Alongside this book, there were two other key outcomes arising from this first phase of development of the International Working Group on Peace Building with Young Children. The first is a clear statement of purpose and objectives for the International Working Group as outlined on the following three pages. As described in this chapter, this has emerged slowly and carefully from the shared experiences and perspectives of early childhood professionals from many different societies impacted by conflict. It provides a clear focus and framework to guide the activities of the International Working Group during its next phase of development.

The second key outcome has been the establishment of a web site — www.peacebuildingwithyoungchildren.org — that provides a focal point for the International Working Group. Further information on the group, including its terms of reference and current activities and events, are provided on the web site as is the opportunity to make contact with and participate in the work of the International Working Group. The International Working Group is developing quickly and it is anticipated that a number of new projects and activities will be launched during 2007 and beyond. You are, therefore, invited to log onto the web site for an update on the work of the International Working Group since preparing this book.

International Working Group on Peace Building with Young Children
Position Paper

Who we are

International Working Group on Peace Building with Young Children is a global initiative by early childhood practitioners, researchers, and civil society organisations, initiated by World Forum Foundation in collaboration with NIPPA – The Early Years Organisation to make visible the role of early childhood development as a force for reconciliation and peace building in regions

Our mission

To be a meeting place for early childhood development activists with an interest in building networks of knowledge, support, and advocacy for early childhood practice and policies in regions experiencing or emerging from armed conflict.

Our goals

- *Transformation* — creating places where, and from which, action and change emanate;

- *Breaking through silences* — raising awareness, giving children and citizens a voice locally, nationally, regionally, and internationally;

- *Reconciliation* — creating places that model interactions which move beyond forgiving and encompass collaboration, partnerships, and building community;

- *Healing* — creating safe places that support children and families and the adults who work with them reach across and through barriers;

- *Building capacity* — providing strategies, skills, and competencies that empower adults working with young children in regions experiencing or emerging from armed conflict.

Our processes

The International Working Group on Peace Building with Young Children is an initiative of the World Forum Foundation and is supported by an *Executive Committee* comprised of members from the World Forum Foundation, NIPPA — The Early Years Organisation (Northern Ireland), and CINDE (Centro Internacional de Educacion y Desarrollo Humano [Colombia]). The Executive Committee oversees the development of a strategic plan detailing the roles and responsibilities and sustainability strategy for the International Working Group.

The *International Working Group* reports to the Executive Committee and comprises the members who are drawn from early childhood practitioners and academics with experience of working in or supporting early childhood programs in regions experiencing or emerging from armed conflict.

Ad-Hoc Committees are formed by members of the International Working Group to take forward priority work areas including advocacy, membership, communications and information, programmatic development, and mobilisation.

Membership — wider membership of the International Working Group on Peace Building with Young Children is open to anyone who is interested in the role of early childhood education as a force for reconciliation and peace building in regions experiencing or emerging from armed conflict. Members will receive regular updates and will be encouraged to participate in activities and events organised by the International Working Group.

Our works

Information dissemination

To raise awareness of the impact of conflicts on children and families and strategies for addressing these.

- Disseminate information and collective experiences from the work of International Working Group on Peace Building with Young Children

- Disseminate information related to the role of ECD in regions experiencing or emerging from conflict.

Sustained linkages

To build the capacity of ECD organisations working in regions experiencing or emerging from conflict.

- Build on inter-personal linkages within the team and build relationships externally

- Document experiences, approaches, strategies, and lessons learned and facilitate sharing models of good practice of work with children and families

- Strengthen links with and between organisations that can provide expertise and skills in the development of conflict sensitive programs that address the needs of children and families.

Advocacy

To raise awareness and support ECD sectors in regions experiencing or emerging from conflict, engage in advocacy campaigns within the sector, and seek out and become involved in campaigns collaboratively with other sectors.

- Adopt and institutionalise a rights-based approach to development

- Regional advocacy campaigns by ECD sector to highlight the nature and impact of conflict on families and children

- Regional advocacy campaigns for greater participation of civil society organisations in the ECD sector in conflict prevention and resolution

- International advocacy campaign by the ECD sector to highlight the global issues related to conflict

- Ongoing exploration of issues and dissemination of ideas at the biennial conference World Forum on Early Care and Education

Mobilization

To take visible and timely action during intense conflict periods to highlight the effects of conflict on children and young families in regions experiencing armed conflict.

- Mobilise support for children and young families in regions experiencing armed conflict Undertake regional media and public policy strategies to raise awareness of the terrible effects of conflict on children and families

Programmatic development

To design new programs that support innovation and evidence in the field of peace building in early childhood care and education in regions experiencing or emerging from armed conflict.

- Contribute to training, advice, and mentoring programs for adults (parents, teachers, and community activists) who support young children in regions experiencing or emerging from armed conflict

- Develop curriculum and resources for young children in regions experiencing or emerging from armed conflict

- Contribute to the research and evidence base on peace building with young children in regions experiencing or emerging from conflict

Postscript

One of the key questions which has driven the development of this book is: "What role can we, as early years professionals, play in terms of helping to build the peace?" By Chapter Ten, we have shown irrevocably that the early years sector has an important role to play locally, nationally, and internationally in advocating for children and bringing pressure to bear for peace.

Early childhood professionals and workers from around the world do not necessarily define their field in the same way. They have wide-ranging goals, diverse methods, and ways of working. There are huge disparities in the early childhood sector in relation to access to resources. Every early childhood professional, trainer, and advocate faces distinct issues which demand vastly different approaches for success. Can we really expect early childhood professionals to work as a united front towards a goal as broad as "bringing pressure to bear for peace"?

The answer is yes.

This book is a direct outcome of the International Working Group on Peace Building with Young Children. The book evolved because of consistent and powerful leadership by the original organisers, and the commitment and mutual support felt by team members. The International Working Group will be making a series of presentations about the contents of this book and the processes that can give voice and power to working groups. The International Working Group represents a sustainable forum for all of us who care about what is happening to young children and who believe that there are windows of opportunities — even within the most drastic situations, where a difference can be made. It is our hope that many more individuals will join the group and work with us. There are many more stories to share, many more learnings to extract, and many more ways that early childhood professionals can make that difference — *together!*

Contributors

International Working Group on Peace Building with Young Children

This listing reflects the groups as organized for Working Forum Belfast and the creation of this book.

Authors

Paul Connolly, Northern Ireland

Paul Connolly is a Professor of Education at Queen's University Belfast. He has researched and published extensively on issues relating to diversity and equality in the early years. His books include: *Boys and Schooling in the Early Years* (2004, RoutledgeFalmer), *Too Young to Notice?: The Cultural and Political Awareness of 3-6 Year Olds in Northern Ireland* (2002, Community Relations Council), and *Racism, Gender Identities and Young Children* (1998, Routledge). Professor Paul Connolly has written a number of articles on the conflict in Northern Ireland and its impact on very young children. His book *Too Young to Notice* suggests that "some children will undoubtedly develop quite entrenched sectarian beliefs at a very young age." Further information on his research and publications can be found at www.paulconnolly.net.

Jacqueline Hayden, Australia

Jacqueline Hayden is Associate Professor of Social Sciences and a fellow of the Research Centre for Social Justice and Social Change at the University of Western Sydney, Australia. She has worked in the area of early childhood in many nations and continents. Some of her recent work involves the development of programs for vulnerable and displaced children in Mauritius and in Rwandan refugee camps; researching young children who have been affected and infected by HIV/AIDS in Namibia; and consulting on early year school programs for indigenous children in Australia. Dr. Hayden has published widely. Titles include

Landscapes in Early Childhood Education: Cross National Perspectives — A Guide for the New Millennium (Peter Lang), and *HIV/AIDS and the Young Child* (University of Namibia Press).

Diane Levin, United States

Diane E. Levin, Ph.D., is a Professor of Education at Wheelock College in Boston, Massachusetts. An internationally recognized expert on helping educators and parents deal with the effects of violence and media and commercial culture on children, Dr. Levin is the author of six books including the newly revised *Teaching Young Children in Violent Times: Building a Peaceable Classroom* and *Remote Control Childhood? Combating the Hazards of Media Culture*. She is a co-founder of Teachers Resisting Unhealthy Children's Entertainment (TRUCE; www.truceteachers.org), an advocacy group which works to promote non-violent, creative play and media (www.truceteachers.org), and Stop Commercial Exploitation of Children (SCEC; www.commercialexploitation.org). Her work has been covered widely in the media including on CNN, Good Morning America, National Public Radio, NBC Nightline, and The New York Times. Dr. Levin has spoken to professional and parent groups around the world, testified before the U.S. Senate Commerce Committee on how violence marketed to children harms them, and has been an advisor for several Public Broadcasting System projects including its parent web site, "Talking to Kids about War and Violence." She has been a participant at the last three World Forums on Early Care and Education.

Organising Team

**Bonnie Neugebauer,
World Forum Foundation**
Bonnie Neugebauer is Vice President of the World Forum Foundation and editor of *Exchange* magazine and Exchange Press Books. She directs program development for the World Forum on Early Care and Education and the Working Forums and provides editorial oversight for www.ChildCareExchange.com and *ExchangeEveryDay*, a daily newsbrief. She has edited many books including: *Alike and Different: Exploring Our Humanity with Young Children, The Art of Leadership, The Wonder of It: Exploring How the World Works,* and *The Anti-Ordinary Thinkbook.* Bonnie is also a writer and photographer for *Exchange* publications. She has presented keynotes and workshop sessions throughout the United States and in several other countries.

**Roger Neugebauer,
World Forum Foundation**
Roger and his wife Bonnie publish *Exchange* magazine. *Exchange* is distributed to 30,000 early childhood leaders worldwide. He is the coordinator of *ExchangeEveryDay*, an  electronic newsbrief, which goes out to 20,000 ECE professionals five days a week. Nine years ago Bonnie and Roger, along with Carmel and Rodney Kenner, conceived the idea of the World Forum.

Siobhan Fitzpatrick, NIPPA
Siobhan Fitzpatrick is Chief Executive Officer of NIPPA – The Early Years Organisation in Northern Ireland, the largest voluntary organisation in Ireland. Siobhan has responsibility for early years' policy, strategy, and financial issues for the organisation and plays a key role in advocacy and policy lobbying on behalf of young children, families, and communities.

Pauline Walmsley, NIPPA
Pauline Walmsley is International Project Manager with NIPPA – The Early Years Organisation. She is responsible for implementing NIPPA's international strategy. This includes expanding the opportunities for the  early years' sector to experience best models from elsewhere including High/Scope and Reggio Emilia. She also supports NIPPA's transnational work in strategic partnership with civic society, ECD and other governmental and non-governmental organisations, parents, and local communities in Eastern Europe and beyond. Pauline previously managed the Cross-Border Rural Childcare Project, an innovative action research project providing rural child care solutions in the border region of Northern Ireland and Republic of Ireland. Pauline is strongly committed to the rights of all children to access quality early childhood development opportunities.

Book Project Support

Samantha Kettyle,
NIPPA
IT Support
Samantha Kettyle commenced employment with NIPPA – The Early Years Organisation in June 2004 as International Project Administrator. This role involved support on projects in Eastern Europe (Albania, Belarus, Moldova, and Serbia), the Organisation's Annual Conference, and projects linked with the World Forum on Early Care and Education. She was heavily involved in the organisation of Working Forum Belfast 2004 and also attended the World Forum in Montreal, May 2005. She left NIPPA in November 2006 and moved to Brisbane, Australia.

Maria Cristina Garcia Vesga, Translator,
CINDE, Colombia
Maria Cristina Garcia, psychologist, Ed.D, is director of the research line on child rearing practices and child/youth development at the Social Sciences Doctorate Program run by CINDE and Manizales University in Colombia. She was Executive Director of CINDE for nearly 12 years. Her field of work has been research and practice of projects and programs around the healthy development of children, as well as the evaluation of social development projects and child/youth programs for different organizations. She is also associate professional at INTRAC Oxford, and at present divides her time between research at the doctorate program and independent consultancies on project evaluation. She has acted as translator for publications by INTRAC, UNICEF, CINDE, and the Bernard Van Leer Foundation.

Rapporteurs

Clockwise — starting at top left:

Kathryn Weill, United States

Ena Shaw, NIPPA, Northern Ireland

Jacqueline Hayden, University of Western Sydney, Australia

Isobel McClean, NIPPA, Northern Ireland

Agatha Thapa, Seto Gurans National Child Development Services, Nepal

Lisa Ruth Shulman, United States

Janet Preston, NIPPA, Northern Ireland

Contributing Reporter

Lisa Ruth Shulman, United States
Lisa Ruth Shulman, J.D., serves as COO and Associate Executive Director of International Child Resource Institute, responsible for international and domestic fund development; program development; strategic management and structuring of organization

operations. She is the co-creator of the Global Healthy Child Care (www.globalhealthychildcare.org) and In-Home Care projects implemented in Argentina, Brazil, China, India, South Africa, and Spain. Ms. Shulman is an international trainer and spokesperson on issues of early childhood care and education. Formerly the Vice President of Child Care Action Campaign, she created the innovative project "Child Care and Equality: A Dialogue on the Societal Value for Care" using scenario development planning to envision solutions to the child care deficit.

Working Team Facilitators

Betty Burkes, United States
Betty Jean Burkes is Pedagogical Coordinator — Hague Appeal for Peace (HAP) in partnership with the UN Department of Disarmament Affairs (DDA), New York City, New York. She is responsible for coordinating a peace education project identifying, creating, and sustaining peace education programming in four communities in four countries (Albania, Cambodia, Niger, and Peru). An initial 6-month investigation process resulted in visits to the four countries to uncover culture/country specific approaches to peace-making which could complement the collection of small arms by the UN-DDA. The process involved meeting with educators, youth, community leaders, and others interested in community-building and peace, creating a local diverse team for implementation, and outlining a direction to be written into a proposal. Exciting ideas emerged including a radio program and theater in Niger, puppetry in Cambodia, high school governance project in Albania, and a peace education center for teachers in Peru. The proposal has been funded by the UNIF and other countries and is now entering its two-year implementation phase. Betty is also Consultant/Trainer for Spirit in Action, Amherst, Massachusetts, an innovative program for fostering transformational leadership for social change. She previously directed a Montessori School in Wellfleet, Massachusetts, and was responsible for co-creating and implementing a curriculum based on the foundations of peace education and creating a just community in which all children (and their families) were welcomed and encouraged to develop.

Diane Levin, United States
Please see bioraphy on page 123 in *Authors* section.

Working Team Participants

Marta Arango Nimnicht, Colombia
Marta Arango Nimnicht was born in Colombia and educated there and in the United States where she received a PhD in Education from the University of California in Berkeley. She co-founded CINDE — the International Center for Education and Human Development — and is its Director. CINDE focuses on the development of innovative programmes for the healthy (physical and psychological) development of young children. Marta has become an international advocate of innovative programs for young children and excluded people. She has received a number of awards including the Simon Bolivar award, Columbia's highest award for personal contribution, and was honored by the Inter-American Development Bank at its 1999 meeting for her contributions to Early Childhood Education in the region.

Paul Connolly, Northern Ireland
Please see bioraphy on page 123 in *Authors* section.

N. Urbain Dembélé, Mali

I am Executive Director of Laboratoire des Techniques d'Education pour le Développement, a private society that works with the University of Mali, the Ministry of Education, and many technical and financial partners. Our special interest is education in Mali and elsewhere. I am National Coordinator of ROCARE: Educational Research Network for West and Central Africa (ERNWACA). A board of trustees, a scientific committee, and a pilot committee for each research project are the bodies I work with to achieve the objectives of the network. About 50 researchers are affiliated to ROCARE-Mali. My experience is particularly related to ECCD and basic education in general. My experience in training and evaluation started while working as an inspector of English and director of Language Laboratories in Mali. In addition to textbook and programme evaluation, I was administrator of CIRSSED in Lomé, Togo, where evaluation was part of the programme I supervised. Since 1993, I have been involved in the evaluation of children and women programmes including designing training modules backed by evaluation tools. My experience extends to Senegal (1998), Ivory Coast (2000), Aga Khan Foundation, UNICEF (Côte d'Ivoire) (1998), UNICEF (Rwanda 2001), OXFAM: Great Britain.

Duane C. Dennis, United States

Duane Dennis has been working in Human Services for the past 22 years. Duane had numerous social work experiences with the Baltimore City Department of Social Services. Of those 22 years, he has been an Administrator in Child Care for 12 years. He began his child care career as the Manager of the Baltimore City Department of Social Services Child Care Subsidy Program. He then became the Executive Director of the Baltimore City Child Care Resource Center where he was the founding Executive Director. Most recently, in Southern California he has had two primary positions. He was the Manager in charge of the Family Preservation, Resource and Referral, and Alternative Payment programs with the Pomona Unified School District. Currently, he is the Executive Director of Pathways. Mr. Dennis has presented both nationally and internationally on such topics as: The Impact of Violence on Young Children; A Bicultural Initiative for African Americans and Latinos; Women, Race and Inequality; and Programmatic topics in Child Care Quality, and Child Care Resource and Referral. Duane is involved with several organizations, which promote justice and fairness, especially for those who are disenfranchised in our society. Mr. Dennis has also published the following papers: "Child Care Needs Assessment Study in the Baltimore City Empowerment Zone" (August 1996); "Child Care in a Community of Violence," et al. (1993).

Andrew Ikupu, Papua New Guinea

My name is Andrew Ikupu. I am a 50-year old man from a country called Papua New Guinea which is in the southwest Pacific region. Over the last 10 years, I have been part of an education reform in my country. As the Superintendent of Elementary Education in my country, I am responsible for establishing preschools all over my country to provide educational access for the six- to eight-year-old children. Over the last decade, children in many parts of my country are exposed to civil unrest mainly due to a civil war in Bouganville (a province of my country), and now ongoing tribal wars in the Highlands provinces. In addition to these problems, our villages and cities are experiencing criminal activities that are very similar to the "wild west" movies we see about the history of the United

States of America. Violence is a part of most children's lives in my country. By establishing the preschools in every community, we hope to address violence through vernacular literacy schools. Although, we do not have money and technical expertise, we are doing our best to provide peace education in any way we can. When I return next year, we will focus on educating young parents. We hope to break the cycle of violence in this manner.

Ingrid Jones, Albania

I have worked for humanitarian and development organizations in Eastern Europe and the Balkans for over five years. Currently I work for Christian Children's Fund, Inc. and I am based in Tirana, Albania, but also have responsibility to develop programmes in Ukraine, Serbia, Moldova, and Belarus as well as in Albania. I have now worked in five countries: Romania, Bulgaria, Kosovo, Russia, and Albania and continue to be amazed and comforted by the resilience, creativity, and motivation I have found amongst the people I am fortunate to work with. My work has consisted of developing social work programmes; training NGO and local government employees; setting up community projects; undertaking research into the needs and services available for ethnic minority children, youth, and families in isolated enclaves; working towards peace, reconciliation, and harmony amongst ethnic minority groups following conflict; ensuring that children's rights are promoted and protected; developing alternative community services for children deprived of their families and destined to a lifetime in large, unfriendly institutions; and latterly looking at the development of regional programmes to assist the most vulnerable and poorest children within Eastern Europe. Within Albania, I am pleased to work on Early Childhood Development Projects, which not only improve the preschool education of children aged three to seven years old, but also to enhance parents' understanding of the health, social, and developmental needs of their babies and young children. Within a backdrop of family and community conflicts, poverty, and surviving, it is often the youngest and most vulnerable, the young children who are the most negatively affected by the adult environment. I am a strong believer in that the west has much to learn from the people we work with in developing countries and that it is not all about teaching and implanting western ideas and methods into inadequate systems, but of a mutual and joint partnership to develop together.

Eleanor Mearns, Northern Ireland

Eleanor Mearns has worked with NIPPA – The Early Years Organisation as an early years specialist for the past 14 years. During that time she has provided support, advice, and training to a range of early years groups in Northern Ireland. Eleanor has been involved in NIPPA's work on "Consulting with Children" both in Northern Ireland and the Republic of Ireland to seek children's views on early years policies. Eleanor is part of NIPPA's "International Division" who are currently developing pre-school provisions in Eastern European Countries. In recent months a substantial part of Eleanor's work has been in the "Media Initiative for Children" which is being developed by NIPPA and the Peace Initiatives Institute (Pii) from the United States. It is a co-ordinated educational programme using a combination of 60-second television messages and pre-school curricula to teach early years children the value of respecting and including others who are different. The three types of differences highlighted in this programme are physical, ethnic, and sectarian. This programme provides young children with an opportunity to openly discuss and acknowledge the feelings associated with similarities and differences between themselves and others. Therefore, it is hoped that children will begin to understand the meaning of acceptance and respect for others leading to inclusion and further peace building.

Ayshe Najjar, Israel

Ayshe Najjar is a Muslim Palestinian Arab of Israeli citizenship. In 1980 Ayshe founded the bilingual/binational preschool in NSWAS. From then until now, she has been in charge of the preschool, which gives children the linguistic and cultural basis to continue on to the NSWAS binational primary school. In the preschool framework, Ayshe has worked with children from the age of three months to the age of six, and has worked most extensively with the kindergarten level (ages four to six). Ayshe created a balanced Hebrew-Arabic educational framework. She continues to participate in enrichment and in-service programs of the Ministry of Education and other frameworks. Ayshe has presented the methods used in the NSWAS binational preschool locally and internationally. In the 1990s she was active in training a group from Macadonia that wished to establish a bilingual kindergarten in Macedonia for Christians and Muslim ethnic Albanians. The program focused on building cooperation between majority and minority cultures, on developing a bilingual teaching environment, and on creating a framework in which there would be equal expression of and respect for Muslim and Christian religious traditions at the preschool.

Félicien Ntakiyimana, Chad
Félicien Ntakiyimana is currently working in Chad as a UNV Programme Officer, Child Protection for UNICEF Chad. Félicien Ntakiyimana has been in Chad since April 2004. They are currently facing an emergency situation in the Eastern part of the country with refugees from Sudan. Félicien Ntakiyimana was working with partners and counterparts to develop early childhood community based development programmes in refugee camps.

Elisa del Puerto, Philippines
Elisa del Puerto made it her personal mission to work with and for the poor families in the different municipalities in Basilan. In 1990, she became Project Manager of Maluso Project affiliated  with Christian Children's Fund (CCF), an international agency devoted to the development of children and the protection of their rights. Much of her attention has been focused on the delivery of social services to more than a thousand children. An offshoot of the Maluso Project is the Maluso Outreach Program, which was sparked by Elisa and supported by Basilan Bishop Romulo de la Cruz. The purpose of the project is to extend help to far-flung areas where children live under the condition of armed conflict. War torn areas have been rehabilitated through the construction or repair of dwellings, bridges, day care centers, and a mosque. Married to a military man, Col. Manuel del Puerto, Elisa courageously faces the challenge of living dangerously in the province of Basilan. She has been instrumental in mediating warring forces for the sake of peace and improving the lives of indigent families. Elisa values education as an essential key in obtaining peace and progress in Basil. At present, Elisa is overseeing the needs of almost 4,000 families, most particularly the children around Basilan. She hopes that the program for children will continue to cover more and more children so that a better and more child-friendly Basil is a realization in the near future.

Radmila Rangelov-Jusović, Bosnia and Herzegovina
Radmila Rangelov-Jusović, Executive Director of Center for Educational Initiatives Step by Step, an organization established with an aim to promote child-centered education and equal rights for quality education for all children in Bosnia and Herzegovina and former president of International Step by Step Association.

Norma Rudolph, South Africa
I am a South African child rights activist with 30 years of experience in education and development in a wide variety of contexts, including government and non-government organisations (NGO), rural and urban;  Early Childhood Development; design and delivery of Teacher Development and Adult Education programmes; classroom practice in primary and secondary schools. My primary interest is in participatory evaluation, training, and strategic project development using participatory action research, a human rights approach to programming and Appreciative Inquiry.

Ali Shaar, Palestine
Ali Nashat Shaar is a senior public health expert with a special focus on mother and child health issues. He has advanced expertise in health promotion and quality improvement. He works with different operational and academic institutions at local and international levels. He has a special interest in early childhood care and development, both as part of his field of expertise, but also as an area of personal passion.

Kishor Shrestha, Nepal
Kishor Shrestha, Ph.D. in early childhood education, is Associate Professor at the Research Centre for Educational Innovation and Development (CERID), Tribhuvan University, Kathmandu, Nepal.
For more than 20 years he has been involved in conducting research, training, and innovative activities in the field of early child care and education in Nepal. He is the coordinator of Early Childhood Development Resource Centre at CERID. He is one of the executive board members of Children First, a national non-governmental

organization working for the welfare and development of children living in disadvantaged situations. He has published numerous articles on early childhood care, education, media, and violence. Dr. Shrestha has presented papers at many national and international conferences. He has served as a consultant to various early childhood development projects run by the Department of Education/Ministry of Education/His Majesty's Government of Nepal, Plan Nepal, Save the Children US, UNICEF Nepal, and local non-governmental organizations.

Aleksandra Selak Zivkovic, Croatia

Aleksandra Selak Zivkovic is currently the Program Director of the NGO "Centre for Social Policy Initiatives" — Centre for the Rights of the Child which included the following programs: Separated Children in Europe Program, Prevention of Child

Trafficking Program, Foster Care Program — Training of Trainers and Foster Parents, BBBS Program and Child Participation in Institutions. Previously she worked with Radda Barnen as the Swedish Save the Children consultant in Albania — developing the Project "Unaccompanied Children in Exile." She served as Project Director, Unaccompanied Children in Exile (UCE); UNICEF Consultant in Bosnia and Herzegovina — Project "Unaccompanied Children in Exile"; Deputy Director of the Project "Unaccompanied Children in Exile"; Programme Officer — UNICEF Croatia; Director of the Regional Institute for Social Welfare — Zagreb; and Association of Trade Unions of Croatia — Advisor for Social Policy for Women and Children.

Working Team Belfast gathered for
"Building Bridges: Healing Communities through Early Childhood Education"
November 17-20, 2004 in Belfast, Northern Ireland

References

Alvarado, S. V., Ospina, H. F., et al. (Julio-Diciembre 2005). "Concepciones de justicia en niños y niñas que habitan en contextos urbanos violentos." En: Revista Latinoamericana de Ciencias Sociales, Niñez y Juventud. Revista del Centro de Investigaciones y Estudios Avanzados en Niñez, Juventud, Educación y Desarrollo, Convenio Universidad de Manizales y CINDE. Vo. 3. No. 2.

Andvig, J. C. (2000). "An essay on child labour in Sub Saharan Africa." Working Paper No. 613, Norwegian Institute of International Affairs.

Arango, M., y Nimnicht, G. (1990). "Participación de los Padres en la creación de Ambientes Adecuados para el Sano desarrollo de los niños." CINDE, Medellín.

Arango, M., Millán, N., Usuga, L. M., y Acosta, A. (1992). "Creación de ambientes adecuados para la prevención de la violencia en la niñez y en la juventud: el caso de La Maruchenga." Presentado en el Taller Internacional sobre Estrategias para Trabajo con La Niñez en Situación de Violencia Nacional. CINDE. Bogotá.

Armenian, H. K. (1989). "Perceptions from epidemiological research in an endemic war." *Social Science and Medicine, 28*(7): 643-7.

Armstrong, S. (2002). "Out of the ashes." *Chatelaine, 75*(2): 65.

Ayalon, O. (1998). "Community healing for children traumatized by war." *International Review of Psychiatry, 10*(3): 224.

Bargo, M. (July/August 2005). "Ripples moving outward: The human impacts of war." *The Humanist*, 35-37.

Barjaba, K. (2004). "Albania: Looking beyond borders." *Migration Information Source.* www.migrationinformation.org/Feature/display.cfm?id=239. Accessed: September 3, 2006.

Bellamy. (1986).

Berkowitz, S. J. (2003). "Children exposed to community violence: The rationale for early intervention." *Clinical Child and Family Psychology Review, 6*(4): 293-302.

Bernstein, C. (2004). "Refugee camp life difficult for the children." www.christianchildrensfund.org/content.aspx?id=421. Last accessed August 20, 2006.

Blair, J. (2004). "Education elusive for children from war-ravaged nations." *Education Week, 23*(25): 11.

Boal, F. (1999). "From undivided cities to undivided cities: Assimilation to ethnic cleansing." *Housing Studies, 14*: 585-600.

Bonilla, R., y González, J. I. (Coordinadores). (Junio 2006). "Bienestar y Macroeconomía 2002-2006: El crecimiento inequitativo no es sostenible." Contraloría General de la República, Centro de Investigaciones para el Desarrollo, CID, de la Universidad Nacional de Colombia. Bogotá.

Botero, P., et al. "Un modelo integral de Educación Básica Rural. Municipio de Balboa — Risaralda." Ministerio de Educación Nacional. Organización de Estados Americanos, OEA. PRODEBAS. Serie Documentos de Trabajo, No 7. Asesoría Técnica CINDE. OP Gráficas. Bogotá. Diciembre.

Brown, B. V., Ph.D., & Bzostek, S. (August 2003). "Violence in the lives of children." *Child Trends Data Bank, 1*: 1-13.

Bryce, J., Walker, N., Ghorayeb, F., & Kanj, M. (1989). "Life experiences, response styles and mental health among mothers and children in Beirut, Lebanon." *Social Science and Medicine, 28*(7): 685-95.

Cairns, E. (1996). *Children and political violence.* London: Blackwell.

Cañabate Lamus, D. (Sin fecha). "Relatos de la violencia, impactos en la niñez y la juventud." Docencia e investigadora IEP-UNAB. Colombia.

Canada, G. (1996). *Fist, Stick, Knife, Gun.* Boston, MA: Beacon Press.

Canada, G. (2002). *Reaching up to manhood: Transforming the lives of boys in America.* Amherst, MA: University of Massachusetts.

Cárdenas Rivera, M. E. (Coordinator). (2003). "La construction del Post-conflicto en Colombia." Enfoques desde la pluralidad. CEREC – FESCOL, Frederich Ebert Stiftung en Colombia. CESO. UNIJUS. Impreso en Prisma Asociados, Bogotá, Colombia.

Carlton-Ford, S. (2004). "Armed conflict and children's life chances." *Peace Review, 16*(2),185-191.

CCF Chad (2006). *Knowledge, attitudes and practices survey: Eastern Chad* www.christianchildrensfund.org/uploadedFiles/Public_Site/news/Relief_professionals/KAP_Chad.pdf. Last accessed August 20, 2006.

CINDE. (1994). Informes Generales de Avance del Proyecto de desarrollo integral La Maruchenga. Equipo Asesor. Medellín.

Concern for Child Workers in Nepal (CWIN). (2006). *Children in armed conflict (a leaflet).* Kathmandu, Nepal: Author.

Concern for Child Workers in Nepal (CWIN). (no date). *Programs on children in armed conflict (a leaflet).* Kathmandu, Nepal: Author.

Conferencia Episcopal de Colombia, Secretariado Nacional de Pastoral Social – Caritas Colombiana, Movilidad Humana. (2006). "Sistematización Proyecto Iglesia y desplazados: Encuentro Solidario." Investigadores: Babativa, Luz María. Briceño, Patricia y Garzón, Juan Carlos. CINDE. ARFO Editores e impresores. Ltda. Bogotá, Colombia. Enero.

Connolly, P., & Healy, J. (2004). *Children and the conflict in Northern Ireland: The experiences and perspectives of 3-11 year olds.* Belfast: Office of the First Minister and Deputy First Minister.

Connolly, P., Smith, A., & Kelly, B. (2002). *Too young to notice? The cultural and political awareness of 3-6 year olds in Northern Ireland.* Belfast: Community Relations Council.

Connolly, P., Fitzpatrick, S., Gallagher, T., & Harris, P. (2006). "Addressing diversity and inclusion in the early years in conflict-affected societies: A case study of the Media Initiative for Children — Northern Ireland." *International Journal for Early Years Education, 14*(3): 263-278.

Derluyn, I., Broekaert, E., Schuyten, G., & De Temmerman E. (2004). "Post-traumatic stress in former Ugandan child soldiers." *The Lancet, 363,* 861-863.

Diario El Espectador. (2000). Bogotá, Colombia, 11 de Julio.

Diario El Tiempo. (2003). Bogotá, Colombia, 25 de Mayo.

Djeddah, C. (1996). "Children and armed conflict." *World Health, 49*(6): 12.

ECPAT. (2006).

El Tempo. (2003).

EMSC. (no date). "After the emergency is over: Post-traumatic stress disorder in children and youth." *Emergency Medical Services for Children Program.* United States Government Human Resources and Safety Administration. www.traumanursesoc.org/pdf/ig_posttrauma.pdf. [As Downloaded 9/6/06].

Eron, L., & Slaby, R. (1994). "Introduction." In Eron, L., Gentry, J. & Schlegel, P. (Eds.). *Reason to hope: A psychological perspective on youth and violence.* Washington, DC: American Psychological Association.

Fay, M., Morrissey, M., & Smyth, M. (1999). *Northern Ireland's Troubles: The human costs.* London: Pluto Press.

Forero, E. (2003). "El desplazamiento interno forzado en Colombia." Ponencia en el Encuentro: "Conflict and Peace in Colombia: Consequences and perspectives for the Future," organizado por Kellog Institute, Woodrow Wilson Internacional Center for Scholars y Fundación Ideas para la Paz. Washington, DC.

Francis, D. J. (2006). "International conventions and the limitations for protecting child soldiers in post-conflict societies in Africa." Paper presented at conference: *Phase II: Protection: Children and War: Impact, Protection and Rehabilitation.* January 14-15, 2006, Los Angeles, California. Accessed 15th August 2006, from www.arts.ualberta.ca/childrenandwar/papers/Children_and_War_Phase_II_Report.pdf.

Fulci, F. P. (1998). "Massacre of the innocents." *United Nations Chronicle, 35*(4): 26.

Gallagher, T. (2001). "Conflict and young people in Northern Ireland: The role of schools," pp. 51-68. In Smyth, M. & Thomson, K. (Eds.). *Working with children and young people in violently divided societies: Papers from South Africa and Northern Ireland.* Belfast: Community Conflict Impact on Children.

Garbarino, J. (1999). *Lost boys: Why our sons turn violent & how we can save them.* New York: Free Press.

Garbarino, J., Dubrow, N., & Kostelny, K. (1991). *No place to be a child: Growing up in a war zone.* Lexington, MA: Lexington Books.

Garbarino, J., Dubrow, N., Kostelny, K., & Pardo, C. (1998). *Children in danger: Coping with the effects of community violence.* San Francisco: Jossey-Bass Publishers.

Garcés, M. P. Escuela Abierta y Autogestionada. Barrio La Maruchenga Bello. Ministerio de Educación Nacional . Organización de Estados Americanos, OEA. PRODEBAS. Serie Documentos de Trabajo. No 6. Asesoría Técnica CINDE. OP Gráficas. Bogotá. Diciembre.

Grupos Investigadores y Organizaciones no Gubernamentales de Colombia. (2000). "Informe de los Grupos investigadores y organizaciones no gubernamentales de Colombia al Comité de los Derechos del Niño." Bogotá, Colombia.

Guha-Sapir, D., & Gijsbert, W. (2004). "Conflict-related mortality: An analysis of 37 datasets." *Disasters, 28*(4): 418-428.

Harvey, R. (2003). "Children and armed conflict: A guide to international humanitarian and human rights law." The Children and Armed Conflict Unit and The International Bureau for Children's Rights. Available from www.essex.ac.uk/armedcon/unit/papers/default.html accessed 18/08/2006.

Institute of Human Rights Commission Nepal (IHRICON). (2003). *Children in armed conflict in Nepalese print media.* Kathmandu, Nepal: Author.

Instituto Nacional de Salud. (1994). "Datos WHO Demographic Yearbook 1990." *Boletín Epidemiológico 2*(4): 58-62.

Karki, A. (2003). "A radical reform agenda for conflict resolution in Nepal." In Karki and Seddon, (Eds.) (2003). *The peoples war in Nepal: Left perspectives.* New Delhi, India: Adroit Publishers.

Karki, A., & Seddon, D. (2003). "The people's war in historical context." In Karki and Seddon (Eds.) (2003). *The peoples war in Nepal: Left perspectives.* New Delhi, India: Adroit Publishers.

The Kathmandu Post. (June 27, 2006).

Kenny, M. (2001). "Personal and theoretical perspectives on systemic practice with families affected by civil conflict," pp. 95-106. In Smyth, M. & Thomson, K. (Eds.) (2001). *Working with children and young people in violently divided societies: Papers from South Africa and Northern Ireland.* Belfast: Community Conflict Impact on Children.

Levin, D. (2003). *Teaching young children in violent times: Building a peaceable classroom* (2nd Ed.). Cambridge, MA: Educators for Social Responsibility and Washington, DC: National Association for the Education of Young Children.

Liddell, C., Kemp, J., & Moema, M. (1993). "The young lions — South African children and youth in political struggle." In: L. Leavitt and N. Fox (Eds.). *The Psychological Effects of War and Violence on Children.* Hillsdale, NJ: Lawrence Erlbaum.

MacCormack. (1999).

Machel, G. (1996). *Impact of armed conflict on children: Report of the expert of the Secretary-General, Ms. Grac'a Machel, submitted pursuant to General Assembly Resolution 48/157: United Nations.*

Machel, G. (September 2000). *The impact of armed conflict on children: A critical review of progress made and obstacles encountered in increasing protection for war-affected children."* Paper presented at the International Conference on War-Affected Children. Winnipeg, Canada.

Macksoud, M. (1994). "Children in war." *World Health, 47*(2): 21.

McKeown, A. (2001). "The impact of conflict on children's play in Northern Ireland: Play deprivation — causes and effects," pp. 231-242. In Smyth, M. & Thomson, K. (Eds.) (2001). *Working with children and young people in violently divided societies: Papers from South Africa and Northern Ireland.* Belfast: Community Conflict Impact on Children.

Marshall M. G., & Gurr, T. R. (2005). "Peace and conflict 2005: A global survey of armed conflicts, self-determination movements, and democracy." Center for International Development & Conflict Management, University of Maryland: College Park. Accessed 15th August 2006 from www.cidcm.umd.edu/inscr/PC05print.pdf.

Marshall, M. G. (2005a). "Global trends in violent conflict." In Marshall, M. G., & Gurr, T. R. (2005). *Peace and conflict 2005: A global survey of armed conflicts, self-determination movements, and democracy.* Center for International Development & Conflict Management. University of Maryland: College Park. Accessed 15th August 2006 from www.cidcm.umd.edu/inscr/PC05print.pdf.

Marshall, M. (2005b). "Focus on political instability in Africa." In Marshall, M. G., & Gurr, T. R. (2005). *Peace and conflict 2005: A global survey of armed conflicts, self-determination movements, and democracy.* Center for International Development & Conflict Management, University of Maryland: College Park. Accessed 15th August 2006 from www.cidcm.umd.edu/inscr/PC05print.pdf.

Masumbuko. (2005).

Maxted, J. (2003). "Children and armed conflict in Africa." *Social Identities, 9(1):* 54-68.

McCauley. (2001).

Measure DHS. (2004). "Selected indicators for Chad." www.measuredhs.com/countries/country.cfm?ctry_id=59 Last accessed 06 August 2006.

Ministry of Public Order, Albania. (2002).

Ministry of Social and Family Affairs, Republic of Chad. (2004). "Guide pédagogique et organisationnel de l'encadrement de la petite enfance au Tchad."

Miosso. (1996).

Morrissey, M., & Smyth, M. (2002). *Northern Ireland after the Good Friday Agreement.* London: Pluto Press.

Moss, W. J., Ramakrishnan, M., Storms, D., Henderson Siegle, A., Weiss, W. M., Lejnev, I., & Muhe, L. (2006). "Child health in complex emergencies." *Bull World Health Organization, 84:* 58-64.

Muldoon, O. T. (2004). "Children of the Troubles: The impact of political violence in Northern Ireland." *Journal of Social Issues, 60*(3): 453(416).

Murray, M. (2001). "The therapeutic use of music with children affected by the Troubles in Northern Ireland and the challenges faced by the therapist," pp. 123-136. In Smyth, M. & Thomson, K. (Eds.) (2001). *Working with children and young people in violently divided societies: Papers from South Africa and Northern Ireland.* Belfast: Community Conflict Impact on Children.

Murtagh, B. (2002). *The politics of territory: Policy and segregation in Northern Ireland.* Basingtstoke: Palgrave.

Murtagh, B. (2003) "Territory, research and policy making in Northern Ireland." In O. Hargie and D. Dickson (Eds.). *Researching the Troubles: Social science perspectives on the Northern Ireland conflict.* Edinburgh: Mainstream Publishing.

NAEYC (National Association for the Education of Young Children). (2006). "NAEYC Position Statement of Violence in the Lives of Children." Author. http://naeyc.org/resources/position_statements/psviol98.htm. Date accessed: June 6, 2006.

NCCP (National Center for Children in Poverty). (2006). *Basic facts about low-income children: Birth to age 3, birth to age 6, birth to age 18.* www.nccp.org/fact.html. Date accessed: June 6, 2006.

Nicolai, S., & Triplehorn, C. (March 2003). "The role of education in protecting children in conflict." Humanitarian Practice Network Paper 42.

Ntakiyimana, F. (2004). "Rapport de visite à Abéché et dans les camps de réfugiés à l'Est du Tchad." 17 Mai – 28 Juin 2004, N'djaména, Chad.

Pearn, J. (2003). "Children and war." *Journal of Paediatrics and Child Health, 39*(3): 166-172.

Petit, J. M. (2002). **"Migraciones, vulnerabilidad y políticas públicas."** *Los movimientos poblacionales y su impacto sobre los niños, sus familias y sus derechos.* Conferencia Hemisférica sobre Migración Internacional: Derechos Humanos y Trata de Personas Santiago de Chile.

Pinto, M. E., Altamar, I. M., Lahuerta, Y., Cepeda, Fernando, L., y Mera, A. V. (2004). "El secuestro en Colombia: Caracterización y costos económicos." Documento 257, Junio 9.

Pittenger, J. (2005). *Child-friendly spaces in the Chadian refugee camps.* Martin Masumbuko www.unicef.org/infobycountry/index_30406_html. Last accessed August 20, 2006.

PNUD (2003). "Informe Nacional de Desarrollo Humano 2003: El conflicto, un callejón con salida," página 122. Página Web. www.pnud.org.co/indh2003, 11 de Septiembre.

Project Counseling Services (PCS) y Consejo Noruego para los Refugiados (CNR). (2004). "Informe regional de Colombia: Fronteras." 19 de Mayo. Bogotá, Colombia.

Pynoos, R. S., & Eths, S. (1985). "Children traumatized by witnessing acts of personal violence." In S. Eths and R. S. Pynoos (Eds.) *Post-Traumatic Stress Disorder in Children.* Washington, DC: American Psychiatric Press.

Rangel, A. (Octubre 2004). "Naturaleza y dinámica de la guerra en colombia y sus efectos sobre el medio ambiente." *Foro Nacional Ambiental Proyecto Paz, Guerra y Medio Ambiente en Colombia.* Bogotá, Colombia.

Raj, P. A. (2004). *Maoists in the land of Buddha: An analytical study of the Maoist insurgency in Nepal.* Delhi: Nirala Publications.

Red de Solidaridad Social (RSS). (Septiembre 2003a). "Presentación del Director General en Seminario de Capacitación a funcionarios de la Procuraduría general de la Nación." Bogotá, Colombia.

Red de Solidaridad Social (RSS). (2003b). "Informe al Congreso de la República — Enero 2002 a Febrero 2003." Tomo I, pag. 4, 14 de Marzo. Bogotá, Colombia.

Research Centre for Educational Innovation and Development (CERID). (2006). *Education of internally displaced children: Provisions and challenges.* Kathmandu: Author.

Research Group. (2000).

Ressler, E. M., Boothby, N., & Steinbock, D. J. (1988). *Unaccompanied children: Care and protection in wars, natural disasters and refugee movements.* New York: Oxford University Press.

Rice, K. F., & Groves, B. (2006). *Hope and healing: A caregiver's guide to working with young children affected by trauma*. Washington, DC: Zero to Three Press.

Rizal, D., & Yokota, Y. (2006). *Understanding development, conflict and violence*. New Delhi, India: Adroit Publishers.

Rodríguez, E., y Bodnar, Y. (Mayo 2006). "Caracterización de la población afrocolombiana desplazada." *Lineamientos de política de atención diferenciada*. Corporación para el desarrollo social y empresarial de los pueblos afrocolombianos, ECODESARROLLO — Organización Internacional de Migraciones, OIM. Convenio Interinstitucional No. id0088 — OIM-1. Bogotá.

Romero, G. (1997). "Demografía de la Violencia en Colombia" y del INS (1991) "Accidentes y muertes violentas en Colombia. Un estudio sobre las características y las consecuencias demográficas 1965-1988." San José Marzo. No publicado.

Rubio, M. (1997). "Paz publica." *Programa de Estudios sobre Seguridad, Justicia y Violencia*. Universidad de los Andes. Documento de Trabajo No. 11. Los costos de la violencia en Colombia.

Sack, W. H., Angell, R. H., Kinzie, J. D., & Rath, B. (1986). "The psychiatric effects of massive trauma on Cambodian children: The family, the home and the school." *Journal of the American Academy of Child Psychiatry*, 25: 377-83.

Santos, F. (Octubre 7 2003). "Las minas antipersonal en Colombia: Desafios y respuestas. Discurso vicepresidente Santos sobre minas antipersonal." Discurso del Vicepresidente de la República y Presidente de la Comisión Nacional de Acción Contra las Minas Antipersonal. Bogotá, Colombia.

Sarmiento, A., González, J. I., et al. (2003). "Finanzas públicas, niñez y juventud. Grupo de economía y niñez." *Serie Economía y Niñez*, No. 1. UNICEF, Fundación Antonio Restrepo Barco, Save The Children del Reino Unido y CINDE. La Imprenta Editores Limitada. Bogotá.

Save the Children. (2006). *Rewrite the future: Education for children in conflict-affected countries*. London: Save the Children.

Save the Children Federation. (2003). *Psychosocial Assessment of Palestinian Children*.

Save the Children Norway (SC/Norway). (2006). *Towards fulfilling the children's rights to development and protection*. Kathmandu: Author.

Sharma & Prasain. (2004). "Gender dimensions of the people's war." In M. Hutt (Ed.) *Himalayan people's war*. London: Hurst & Company.

Shulman, L. R. (2006). "The role of early childhood development programs in conflict and post-conflict settings." Paper presented at conference: *Phase II: Protection: Children and War: Impact, Protection and Rehabilitation*. January 14-15, 2006, Los Angeles, California. Accessed 15th August 2006, from www.arts.ualberta.ca/childrenandwar/papers/Children_and_War_Phase_II_Report.pdf.

Smyth, M. (1998). *Half the battle: Understanding the impact of the Troubles on children and young people.* Derry/Londonderry: INCORE.

Smyth, M., & Hamilton, J. (2003). "The human costs of the Troubles." In O. Hargie and D. Dickson (Eds.). *Researching the Troubles: Social science perspectives on the Northern Ireland conflict.* Edinburgh: Mainstream Publishing.

Stohl, R. J. (2002). "Under the gun: Children and small arms." *African Security Review, 11*: 3.

Thomson, K. (2001). "Living in South Africa: The consequences for asylum seeker and refugee children from Africa," pp. 179-197. In Smyth, M. & Thomson, K. (Eds.) (2001). *Working with children and young people in violently divided societies: Papers from South Africa and Northern Ireland.* Belfast: Community Conflict Impact on Children.

Tokar, C. (2006). "Indigenous protections of children in armed conflict: Observations from Sierra Leone and Liberia," pp. 19-24. Paper presented at conference: *Phase II: Protection: Children and War: Impact, Protection and Rehabilitation.* January 14-15, 2006, Los Angeles, California. Accessed 15th August 2006, from www.arts.ualberta.ca/childrenandwar/papers/Children_and_War_Phase_II_Report.pdf.

UNICEF. (1996). "Promotion and protection of the rights of children: Impact of armed conflict on children." Report accessed from: www.unicef.org/graca/a51-306_en.pdf.

UNICEF. (2000). "Graça Machel calls for an end to impunity for war crimes against children and women." Media release accessed 29 August 2006 from www.unicefusa.org/site/apps/nl/content2.asp?c=duLRI8O0H&b=124734&ct=151359.

UNICEF. (2006). *State of the world's children.* Retrieved 3 January, 2006 from www.unicef.org/sowc06.

United Nations. (2002). "Update on children and armed conflict." UN General Assembly Special Session on Children 2002. Available from www.developmentstudies.org/PolicyAdvocacy/pahome2.5.nsf/allreports/740E69E2C2AC561488256E46008 360CE/$file/World%20Vision%20UK%20Children%20and%20Armed%20Conflict%20Update%20UNGASS% 202002.pdf

United Nations. (2006). *Report of the Special Representative of the Secretary-General for children and armed conflict.* Accessed from: www.crin.org/docs/Report_SR_VAC_GA61.pdf.

United Nations Development Programme (UNDP). (2004). *Diber MDG regional development strategy.* Tirana, Albania: Author.

United Nations Development Programme (UNDP) & Sustainable Economic Development Agency (SEDA). (2005). *Pro-poor and pro-women policies and development in Albania: Approaches to operationalising the MDGs in Albania.* Tirana, Albania: Author.

Upreti, B. R. (2004). *The price of neglect.* Kathmandu: Bhrikuti Academic Publications.

U.S. Center for Disease Control and Prevention. (2004). "Emergency nutrition and mortality surveys conducted among Sudanese refugees and Chadian villagers, Northeast Chad." www.cdc.gov/nceh/ierh/ResearchandSurvey/Chad_report04.pdf. Last accessed August 20, 2006.

U.S. Department of Health & Human Services, Administration for Children and Families. (2002). *Head Start Bulletin*, No. 73, www.headstartinfo.org/publications/hsbulletin73/hsb73. 29.htm. Date accessed: June 6, 2006.

U.S. Department of State. (2005). "Background note: Albania." www.state.gov/r/pa/ei/bgn/3235.htm Last accessed: September 3, 2006.

Women's Commission for Refugee Women and Children. (February 2005). *Learning in a war zone: Education in Northern Uganda*. Retrieved 15 December, 2005, from www.womenscommission.org/pdf/Ed_Ug.pdf.

World Forum Foundation. (2004). "Building Bridges: Healing Communities through Early Childhood Education" CD. Redmond, WA: Exchange Press. Order online: www.ChildCareExchange.com. Click on World Forum Foundation.

World Vision. (2004). "Pawns of politics: Children, conflict and peace in northern Uganda." World Vision, accessed 15th August, 2006 from www.worldvision.ca/home/media/PawnsOfPolitics.pdf.

Zwi, A. B., Grove, N. J., Kelly. P., Gayer, M., Ramos-Jimenez, P., & Sommerfeld, J. (2006). "Child health in armed conflict: Time to rethink." *The Lancet, 367*(9526): 1886-1888.

Resources

Connolly, P., Smith, A., & Kelly, B. (2002). "Too Young to Notice? The Cultural and Political Awareness of 3-6 Year Olds in Northern Ireland." Belfast: Community Relations Council. www.paulconnolly.net/publications/report_2002a.htm

Connolly, P., & Healy, J. (2004). "Children and the Conflict in Northern Ireland: The Experiences and Perspectives of 3-11 Year Olds." Belfast: Office of the First Minister and Deputy First Minister. www.paulconnolly.net/publications/report_ofmdfm_2004a.htm

Hopkins, S. (1999). *Hearing everyone's voice: Educating young children for peace and democratic community.* Redmond, WA: Exchange Press.